The Mechanics of Creative Writing

Ben Bennetts

Summary

Do you fancy yourself as a creative writer? Do you enjoy composing great works of literary art—meticulous texts, elegant e-mails, scathing or amusing letters to an editor, scintillating blogs, entertaining short stories, erudite reference books, unputdownable novels? Is there even such a word as *unputdownable*? (There is now!)

Is your grammar up to scratch? Do you copy edit your own compositions? Did you know there are no officially-sanctioned rules for English grammar? There is, however, a multitude of opinions on what constitutes correct usage, incorrect usage, and usage that will attract attention—*to boldly go* springs to mind.

I use what I call the bish-bash-bosh style of creative writing: *bish* the words down into a Word file, *bash* them around, and *bosh* them to perfection. If this is your writing style, do you know how to manipulate your embryonic text into its final magnificent form using the hidden powers of Microsoft Word (Styles, Paragraph Marker, Find and Replace, Spellcheck and Autocorrect)? How about graphics? Do you understand the copyright infringement perils of copying and using images, and text, from websites for use in your scholarly production? Finally, when you've finished creating, do you know how to self-publish as an e-book, or even as a something-to-be-proud-of paperback or hardback book?

So many questions; so little time. Read this book and gain a head start into the heady world of creative writing and self-publishing.

Copyright © 2018, Ben Bennetts

All rights reserved. No part of this publication may be reproduced or transmitted in any form or by any means, electronic or mechanical including photocopying, recording or any information storage or retrieval system, without prior written permission in writing from the publishers.

The right of Ben Bennetts to be identified as the author and illustrator of this work has been asserted by him in accordance with the Copyright, Designs and Patents Act 1988.

Every effort has been made to trace all copyright holders of material, textual and graphic, quoted or otherwise used in this book. Any omissions will be acknowledged and included in future editions if application is made in writing or by e-mail to the author at ben@ben-bennetts.com

First published in the United Kingdom in 2018 by Atheos Books.

ISBN-13: 978-1717407245
ISBN-10: 1717407242

Contents

1. Introduction 1
2. Grammar and Punctuation 11
3. The Basic Tools of Writing 21
4. Copy Edit: Polish, Polish, Polish 30
5. Copyright: the Perils of Copy and Paste 50
6. Publishing your Book: E-book or P-book? 56
7. Creative Writing: Some Final Comments 69
Further reading 71
Acknowledgements 74
About the Author 75
Atheos Books 76
Index 80

Dedication

This book is dedicated to the small army of family and friends who helped me copy edit my earlier books. Like me, they did not find all the mistakes but, ~~liked~~ like me, they tried.

THE MECHANICS OF CREATIVE WRITING

1. Introduction

"Grandpa, where do the stories come from?" asked Nikki, when both she and Tommy were sitting in Grandpa's kitchen one evening after school.

"Oh, I don't know. Tommy has already asked me that question. Out of my head, I guess," replied Grandpa.

"Who put them there?" asked Nikki.

"Nobody that I know of. They just happen."

"Can you tell a story about anything?" said Tommy.

"Pretty much. I just need a few characters or a situation and, bingo, the story starts to take shape. Then, all I require is an audience."

"Don't you write it down first?" asked Nikki.

"No. In fact, I don't think I've ever written down a story before I told it. I might write it down afterwards but then it becomes a different story. I add extra characters, change the plot, add more detail, and so on."

"Yes, but I still don't understand how you can tell the story in the first place," said Nikki.

"Nor me, Nikki, nor me. As I said to Tommy, once I start talking the story 'just happens'. As I talk, I think about what's going to happen next, and so the story continues until I reach the end. Maybe I have a good imagination?"

"Can we have a story now?" asked Tommy.

...

Chapter 11, The Dream Guardian, Ben Bennetts, 2017

THE MECHANICS OF CREATIVE WRITING

I'm sometimes asked, "How do you do it?"

"Do what?" I reply.

"Write all these blogs, stories, books, and oh-so-elegant e-mails. How do you get started? How do you know what to write? Where does the content come from? What's the process?"

"I've no idea," I reply again, "but I'll sure as hell tell you!"

Okay, it's not quite like that but I have been asked how I create blogs and books and I have pondered on the process of what many people call 'creative writing'. But, what do we mean by creative writing? A simple definition is anything that has not been written (created) before but that definition collapses if I was to offer *The cat donned a purple coat and ate an apple before embarking on his world tour.* I'm sure nobody has ever written this sentence before but is it creative? It depends on what follows.

The Concise Oxford Dictionary defines creative as an adjective *relating to or involving the use of imagination or original ideas in order to create something.* My sentence fits this definition but would it hold your attention and motivate you to continue reading? Maybe; maybe not.

Creative writing is more than just stringing words together in a way that intrigues, stimulates, and causes enjoyment. It's about writing something that endures over time and gives some sort of long-lasting pleasure to the reader. The Brontë sisters knew how to do it, as did William Shakespeare, Charles Dickens, Agatha Christie, Arthur Conan Doyle and a host of other now-deceased writers. John le Carré knows how to do it. Dan Brown, Robert Ludlum, Patricia Cornwell, Stephen King, Danielle Steel, Ken Follett... they all know how to spin a yarn that'll keep you turning the pages. Hilary Mantel, maybe. (I have difficulty with Hilary Mantel's complex intertwined plot lines but she sure knows how to write.) Some of these authors may not be to our liking but they certainly know how to be creative.

My personal journey of writing creatively started way back in the early 1950s when I wrote a report on my jungle camping expedition with the RAF Negombo Jungle Rescue team. We spent a weekend camping close to the town of Kurunegala in Sri Lanka (known as Ceylon in the '50s when I lived there). I was ten years old and my rank in the Boy Scout Wolf Cubs' pack entitled me, and two others from the pack, to join the 3-day simulation exercise. It was great fun and I still have my report complete with spelling mistakes, strange punctuation, and an unusual use of the colon (Mr: Smith's dog, Rex...). I recall that my father helped me put my report together but the 1,300 words were mine. I'm proud of it!

THE MECHANICS OF CREATIVE WRITING

At secondary school, I was not especially motivated to write anything other than was required to support my schoolwork. I achieved a pass in O-level English Language but was not enamoured by the rules of English grammar. I started reading novels, however, by authors such as Ray Bradbury, Dennis Wheatley, Edgar Allan Poe, Isaac Asimov, Arthur Conan Doyle, Walter Scott, Robert Louis Stevenson, Herman Melville, and, of course, William Shakespeare. My thirst for 'a good read' was insatiable and I came to appreciate how an author could unravel a story, introduce strange and provocative concepts (especially the sci-fi authors), and keep me glued to the pages rather than be out and about on the sports field or chasing after the girls from the local girls' school. I was a bookworm. I was a reader, but not an author or a writer. (There's a difference. An author originates ideas, event sequences, and storylines, whereas a writer converts the work of the author into words, sentences, paragraphs and, ultimately, creates a complete literary work. Not all authors are writers, and vice versa.)

Throughout my university study years, I wrote very little; an occasional letter, some scrappy lecture notes, some project reports and end-of-course theses, and that was about it. The theses were highly technical, full of Boolean mathematics, and did not lend themselves to any form of what we might call creative English. This very rigid style of writing continued as I commenced my career in the electronics industry, first as a university lecturer (1972 - 1979) and then as an engineer and consultant in electronics and a presenter of short courses (1979 - 2007). At the beginning of my career, I started writing and publishing technical papers on my specialist subject, not paying too much attention to grammatical accuracy or literary appeal. All I cared about was that the technical content was correct and the paper was suitable for publication. Kudos was everything!

Then, in 1974, something traumatic happened. I'd submitted a technical paper to an American professional journal and the editor, Ralph Evans, wrote to me asking for some grammatical revisions. In his letter, Ralph wrote:

"Thank you for your contribution. Technically it's fine but grammatically you do have a tendency to use the indefinite pronoun with an unclear antecedent."

I was taken aback. What on earth was the indefinite pronoun? What was meant by its antecedent? How dare an American tell me, an Englishman, that I could not write in my native language correctly?

Well, he did dare, and I couldn't write properly!

THE MECHANICS OF CREATIVE WRITING

Ralph's words challenged me first to find out what he meant and second to make sure I would never again be accused of writing sloppy English. I sought help. I spoke with a fellow lecturer asking what book he would recommend for me to refresh my knowledge of my untouched-since-schooldays English grammar. He grabbed his copy of *The Complete Plain Words* by Gowers and Fraser, thrust it into my hand and suggested I buy a copy. This I did from the University bookshop. My copy was published in 1973 but the origin of the book dates back to just after World War Two.

It's a crackerjack book and ever since this incident I have sought to make sure that my written words are grammatically correct and unambiguous in meaning. I now have almost twenty books on English grammar on my bookshelf and, when in doubt, I consult them. Such is the legacy of Ralph Evans' short note to me in 1974.

Around the year 2000, I started writing non-technical essays for pleasure. It began with what I hoped were elegantly worded e-mails to people in large organisations, usually complaining but sometimes just commenting. Gradually, the subject matter expanded and I diversified into writing opinion pieces on anything that caught my attention—an item in the news, an observation of behaviour, a mathematical or grammatical curiosity—and sending my essays, unsolicited, to family and friends. As I progressed, I began to concentrate more on sentence construction, word selection, grammar, and removal of ambiguity. I sought out alternative ways to express myself. I paid attention to punctuation. I began to beef up my sentences. The cat no longer sat on the mat. Instead, the snowy-white Japanese Bobtail stretched out lazily on the swirly-patterned easy chair.

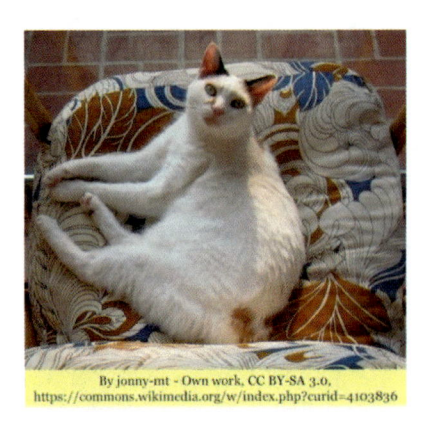

By jonny-mt - Own work, CC BY-SA 3.0,
https://commons.wikimedia.org/w/index.php?curid=4103836

I began a closer check on word form and spelling. The Japanese Bobtail stretched out, not the Japanese bobtail or japanese bobtail. I started looking for synonyms to replace repeated words in the same sentence or add flavour to a mundane phrase: the village of Littleton was a ~~village~~ habitation mostly made up of ~~immigrants~~ newcomers. I began hunting for misplaced *only*s. I started purging surplus *also*s. I looked for and removed unnecessary intensifiers and stuffers, words like *really, actually, totally*, and so it went on. I went back to my books on grammar to check or relearn the rules. I sorted out my *thats* from my *whichs*. I started keeping notes on things to watch out for; bad habits, preferred spellings when alternatives exist (*website* or *web site*, *Wi-Fi* or *wifi*, for example). I ramped up a learning curve on various features in Microsoft Word such as Find and Replace, the use of Styles, the built-in Spellchecker, even the paragraph marker (the pilcrow ¶). I became a power user of Word. I used PowerPoint and PaintShop Pro to create and edit images. In short, I was evolving into a writer rather than just a text-only essayist.

The big year was 2012. This was the year I published my first non-technical paperback book, *The Religion Business: Cashing in on God*. I spent eighteen months researching the topic and writing the chapters. It was an intensive exercise and made me realise that writing a 95,000-word book was a whole new experience. I learned about copy editing and proofreading (again, they are different—see later) and I entered into the world of self-publication. I signed up with a hard-copy print-on-demand printing company and complied with the recommended page layout and formatting guidelines. I researched copyright law to make sure I wasn't infringing the copyright of others, either in my use of quotations from other publications or images I copied from various websites.

My second attempt at self-publishing was an extended essay, *Memories of RAF Negombo, 1950 - 1952*, also published in 2012. I used the essay as a vehicle to explore the new world of self-publishing as an e-book, an electronic version of a book that could be read on the screen of a computer or tablet reader. This led me to an understanding of the differences between publishing in hard-copy and soft-copy forms. E-books have no page numbers but page layout is still important if the book is to display properly on an e-reader's screen. In the essay, I experimented with embedded graphical images—size, resolution, position, colour—and the use of bookmarks and hyperlinks to navigate the book. It was all good fun and, to date (2018), the essay has been downloaded over a thousand times and led to a reunion in 2014 with one of my boyhood friends from over sixty years ago.

Ceylon (Sri Lanka) Circa 1951

UK 2014

    Since the publication of the two 2012 works, I have added a further ten books, all as e-books and some as printed books (p-books). I've written books that detailed my life as a consultant electronics engineer, my adventures walking long-distance trails, a republication of a 1977 booklet on home-made winemaking, a work of fiction containing erotic content (writing under a pseudonym), two collections of short essays on a wide variety of topics, a book on the quirks of some of the words in the English language, and my most recent book, a storybook for children.

    Experimenting with these different genres has expanded my creativity as an author, and refined my skills as a writer. It's always difficult to know exactly where you stand in the ranks of creativity—who's to judge?—but I enjoy writing. I enjoy creating something that will give pleasure to others when they read it—maybe some humour, maybe a new insight, maybe raise some hackles, maybe impart some knowledge—and judging by the feedback offered to me by my readers, I have achieved some of these results.

    My objective in this book is to write about the mechanics (tools and techniques) to enable and support creative writing based on my own journey of discovery. Any artist—a painter, a sculptor, a composer of music—must first know how to use the tools and understand their constraints. Just as a tree carver cannot carve if the chainsaw blade is blunt, so a writer cannot write without the aid of a dictionary, a thesaurus and, as it turns out, a variety of other tools. In the chapters that follow I will discuss tools and techniques necessary to create a literary work, highlighting some of the basic tricks of the trade. I will concentrate on writing a fiction or non-fiction book containing multiple images and which is destined to become both an e-book and a p-book. This is the most complex form of writing and formatting for publication. If you can do this, writing a letter, an e-mail, a text-only essay or book, or a blog, will all become a doddle!

Here goes...

Getting Started

What do you want to write? An entertaining and well-composed e-mail to a friend or colleague? A letter to an editor? An essay to be published in a magazine or posted on a website (a blog)? A short story? A novel? A technical report? This is your first decision.

What is the nature of the publication? Is it text only, or will it also contain images? Do you want to publish as a hard-copy printed book (abbreviated to p-book) or a soft-copy e-book, or just as a blog which, of course, is a simplified form of an e-book?

Have you got all the necessary tools—a word processor on a computer (or an antiquated typewriter if word processors are not for you), a dictionary, a few books on English grammar just in case, a thesaurus, access to the Web to check facts where necessary, nimble fingers, and an ever-bubbling coffee pot close by?

Finally, you've done all the thinking about what you want to write, and you've sorted out when you will start creating your masterpiece—early in the morning when all is peace and quiet, late at night when the creative juices flow best, during the day when the children are at school. You're ready to go.

The hour arrives. You sit down and in best Hollywood stereotypical fashion, interlink your fingers, bend them backwards to loosen the joints (and make that horrible cracking noise), place them lightly on the keyboard (all ten if you have learned to touch-type, or just four if you're a hunt-and-pecker like me), stare at the screen and... wait... and wait some more... and look up and out of the window hoping for inspiration. That first sentence is always the hardest.

The first sentence is what will open your creative floodgates, entrance and trap the reader, set the tone for what's to come. Beethoven got it right with the opening *dah-dah-dah-da* of his fifth symphony, as did Richard Strauss with the stirring opening crescendo of *Also Sprach Zarathustra* (used with great effect in

THE MECHANICS OF CREATIVE WRITING

Stanley Kubrick's 1968 movie *2001: A Space Odyssey)*. George Orwell hit on an arresting statement with his opening line to *Nineteen Eighty-Four*, "It was a bright cold day in April, and the clocks were striking thirteen." Or what about J M Barrie's opening line to his book, *Peter Pan*: "All children, except one, grow up."

If the opening sentence won't come, don't force it. Have a coffee. Walk the dog. Watch a movie. Just wait. It'll happen in due course. In my case, I retire early and wait! I'm an early riser and often I'll wake with the opening sentence buzzing in my head. That's my cue to get up and start typing.

It's the same with titles. To my mind, a book title should be short, catchy, explanatory, and memorable; an informative attention grabber. *Catch-22* was a great book title, as was *Nineteen Eighty-Four* and *Catcher in the Rye*.

In the case of this book, I knew I wanted *Creative Writing* as part of the title but a search on Amazon revealed many books whose title included those two words so how to differentiate? My initial stab at a title was *Creative Writing: Do Sheep Dream of Humans?*, an inversion of Philip K Dick's *Do Androids Dream of Electric Sheep?* (the book that inspired the cult 1982 movie, *Blade Runner*). This was followed by *Creative Writing: a Journey of Discovery* which survived as a working title until one of my cousins pointed out that the book was more focused on the technicalities of creative writing rather than the elements of creative writing which he described as being topics such as how to develop the interplay of characters; how to structure a piece of writing; what, if any, literary conventions to use (story, poem, play, report…); how to use descriptive dialogue, and so on. My cousin was right. In the end, I settled for *The Mechanics of Creative Writing*. There's enough there to inform and intrigue anyone searching for a book on creative writing and it captures the essence of what the book is about.

Getting the title right, and laying down that first sentence can be tricky. Don't underestimate their difficulty and importance.

Planning

We should talk a bit about planning. At school, or in creative writing classes, we are taught the importance of planning the structure and content of an essay or something larger such as a book. I do plan. I write down chapter headings and the topics to be covered therein. I start researching where necessary. I gather references and links to websites for later perusal and digestion. But, I do not follow the plan religiously. I change it on the fly. In the case of my two anecdotal books on long-distance walking, *Tales from the Trails, Parts 1 and 2*, I spent a considerable amount of time planning which anecdotes I wanted to narrate and in which chapter and book they fitted. Then, when I started writing, not much changed in the structure of the book.

Two years later I wrote my children's book, *The Dream Guardian*. This book is a series of short unrelated bedtime stories with a top-level inter-chapter storyline. The initial plan for the book was very sketchy. At the start, I had no idea how many chapters I wanted to write nor how the main storyline would progress. That book just happened, and that is the nature of creative writing. You cannot ordain how a new book will turn out. Depending on type and genre, the degree of planning will range from virtually nothing to very detailed. Do what you think is necessary to get you started, but be prepared to deviate many times.

The Writing Environment

I'll not say much about this. Some authors like some sort of noise in the background, a murmuring television or soothing music through headphones; others do not. Some like to write in a room set aside for such activities, such as a study or spare bedroom; others are happy to create with a laptop on their knee in a living room. Some can write while travelling on a bus, a train, or an aircraft; others prefer a quiet spot in the home. It's up to you. Find the best environment to stimulate your creative juices and let them flow.

Version Control and Backup File

Make sure you back up your Word file every hour on the hour and keep backup copies on an external memory such as a memory stick. Once the words flow, you will get lost in your own world of brain-to-fingers-to-screen transmission and before you know it, your arm, shoulder and back will ache, and your body will crave caffeinated coffee. You may also need a bio-break! Before you respond to whatever need becomes pressing, back up your file. Give it a version number, if necessary, or just rely on the date and time allocated to the file by your Save function but make an offline copy, just in case. There is nothing more frustrating than to lose an hour's work if Microsoft's Word, Apple's Pages or Apache's OpenOffice Writer suddenly freezes and you have to Ctrl+Alt+Del out of it. If it happens, and you've no backup copy, I can tell you; you will never

THE MECHANICS OF CREATIVE WRITING

recreate exactly what you've just lost. It will be different, maybe better, maybe not, but it will be different. I speak from experience.

Okay, let's get started on the basics.

(^_^)

2. Grammar and Punctuation

English grammar is fascinating. There are no officially-sanctioned rules but there is a multitude of opinions on what constitutes correct usage, incorrect usage and usage that will attract attention—*to boldly go* springs to mind. In the days when I wrote technical papers and textbooks, I tried hard to adhere to what I would now term consensus grammar—grammar we agree is correct by consensus rather than by decree. These days, I occasionally break the rules, usually for effect. When I do this, who is to pronounce judgement and with what authority?

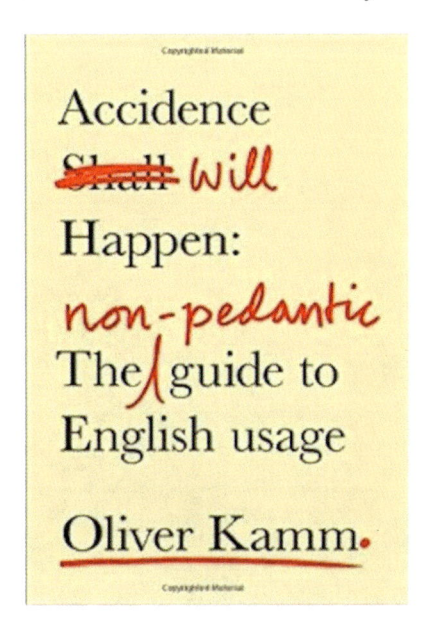

THE MECHANICS OF CREATIVE WRITING

Oliver Kamm hit the nail on the head in his 2015 book *Accidence Will Happen: The Non-Pedantic Guide to English Usage* (Weidenfeld and Nicolson). I enjoyed reading his book (the second time round!) and posted a short opinion piece on my website. Here it is:

Rules is Rules, Right?

Oliver Kamm is a regular contributor to *The Times* newspaper on English usage. He writes a column called Pedant which, as it turns out, is exactly what he's not, or so he claims.

I've read his book, twice. The first time round he made me mad. Second time round, not so mad.

He claims that many English grammar pedants (he calls them sticklers) don't have a leg to stand on when pronouncing judgement on the construction of some English word, phrase or sentence. He says there is no definitive book on the rules of English grammar; no authoritative body set up to maintain the rules; no historical reasons why certain rules should be upheld. He sanctions split infinitives; sentences that start and end with conjunctions and prepositions; claims "I can't get no satisfaction" is acceptable simply because the meaning is clear; and states that evidence of use by famous authors always supersedes what the rule books say.

Is he right? Yes, to a certain extent. There *are* no definitive books on the rules of English grammar. There is a bunch of opinions and judgements however, many published in reputable rulebooks, revered as gospel and quoted chapter and verse by self-proclaimed pedants.

MY BOOKCASE CONTAINING SEVERAL BOOKS ON ENGLISH GRAMMAR

THE MECHANICS OF CREATIVE WRITING

I have some of these books on my bookshelf: books by Fowler, Partridge, Gowers and Fraser, Heffer, Parrish, Strunk and White, Truss, and others. Plus, there are many websites where one can go for grammatical guidance: Grammar Girl, Grammarly, Oxford Dictionary, Daily Writing Tips, for example. Like Kamm, I have found inconsistencies across this spectrum of books and websites and, like Kamm, I break the rules when it suits my style. I boldly split infinitives. And I start sentences with conjunctions plus I don't believe that a preposition is a word that you can't end a sentence with. But, I draw the line at saying "Bill and me went to the shops". I have come to the conclusion that, in the end, how you write is a matter of style coupled with tone—how you want the words to come across to the reader—formal, informal, colloquial, with a twang, with a dialectal resonance. (Kamm calls this matter of style the *register* of the prose.)

His point about phrases such as "Bill and me..." and "Between you and I..." is that although considered incorrect by grammatical mavens, if the sense of what is meant is clear then why should authors, and speakers, be held back by, for example, nominative (subject) and accusative (object) rules that hark back to Latin? Latin is Latin, and dead: English is English, and very much alive, and although one is partly derived from the other, there is no rule that says the derivative language (English) should conform to the grammatical rules of the source language (Latin). If modern usage employs expressions considered by self-appointed grammarians to be incorrect, then so be it. Languages are living things constantly being changed by usage and by many other influences. Two of my granddaughters are forever saying "Me and my friend..." or peppering their speech with the redundant stuffer word *like* (the modern teen version of *um* or *ah*), or using unnecessary adverbial intensifiers such as *really* or *actually*. When challenged as to why they do this, they replied that all their friends at school do it so they do it as well. It's tough to argue with that reply and Kamm would uphold their right to both speak and write in this way. Usage changes the language, he says. Evidence of non-pedantic use supports further non-pedantic use. (Kamm's book is loaded with examples of non-pedantic use taken from the publications of many famous and well-respected authors: Austin, Shakespeare, Dickens, Chaucer, Amis, Brontë, Twain...)

THE MECHANICS OF CREATIVE WRITING

But, we cannot let grammatical anarchy rule supreme. How would anybody learn English as a second language if there were no rules? A language teacher has to put a stake in the ground and select a basic set of rules in order to build a syntactical framework for teaching the language. This means selecting and accepting at least one of the rulebooks to use as a base. Once mastered, the pupil can exercise his or her right to break the rules, as I now do, but there has to be a reference point from which the author can depart. Kamm does not make this observation. He should have done so.

In the past, I have labelled myself a pedant, but I must confess that as my writing expertise has developed I have become bolder in my writing style. But, I usually know when I'm breaking the rules and some will remain inviolate. I could never bring myself to write "I didn't see nobody," for example, when writing in a formal register (as opposed to a colloquial register). Not only is the phrase illogical, to do so makes a mockery of the definition of the word *nobody* as defined in a dictionary. I rely heavily on dictionaries, not just for spellings and meanings but also for uncommon usage. If the meaning of a word changes as, for example, *awesome, wicked*, or *decimate*, then I'm happy to make use of the new meaning but I am careful to ensure that the context makes the new meaning clear. I regard those who compile the entries in dictionaries (lexicographers) to be the guardians of spellings *and* meanings and whereas I am sometimes interested to explore the origins of words (their etymology), I am no longer resistant to new developments in their usage. I accept that languages evolve. Whaddya think?

Kamm has written an interesting book and I have sympathy with many of his observations but I think he could have stressed the need for a base set of rules even though he is critical of many of the books on grammar, and of the army of amateur pedants who voice opinions about usage. His book is also strangely contradictory. He says that evidence of usage transcends any arbitrary rule in a grammar book. That statement, in itself, is a rule and indeed the second half of his book exposes many such usage-supported-by-evidence rules.

If you are an author, blogger, or even just an e-mailer who sometimes struggles to construct a sentence stylishly, unambiguously and correctly (whatever *correctly* now means), you will benefit from reading Kamm's opinions. If you are not an author but have an interest in the progression of English as a language, Kamm's book will add to your understanding of word mutation and language evolution. If you are a dyed-in-the-wool pedant, Kamm's book will annoy you but may cause you to rethink some of your opinions on usage. If you are none of these, Kamm's book is best avoided.

Having said all this, as a creative writer you will need to define your own set of grammatical rules. Do you want to conform to a set of generally accepted rules as laid down in one of the books, Gowers and Fraser for example, or do you want to step outside the rule box, occasionally or dramatically?

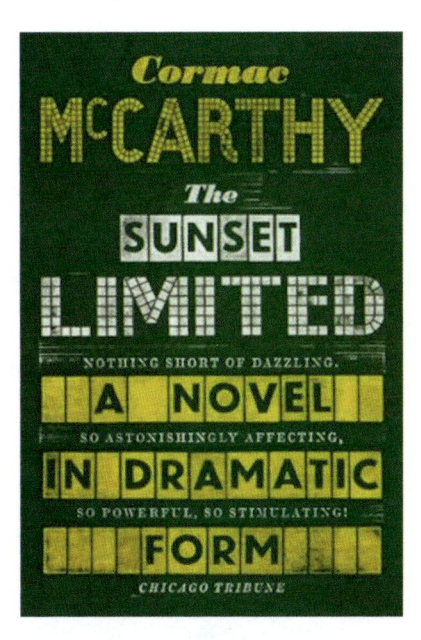

The script for Cormac McCarthy's 2006 play *The Sunset Limited* is an example of stepping outside the box. The play takes place in a small apartment of a black man, Black, who has just prevented a white man, White, from jumping in front of the New Orleans - Los

Angeles Sunset Limited express train. The book details the conversation between the two men, one an atheist (White), the other a believer in God (Black). The dialogue, written in a colloquial style, breaks many so-called basic rules of English grammar and yet is perfectly understandable.

~~~~~

Continuing with the theme of what is right and what is wrong, look at punctuation. We can agonise to the nth degree over where to place a comma, or whether a comma should be an upmarket semicolon or even a full-blown majestic colon. I tend to punctuate according to how the text flows when I read it aloud but I know, and have been told, that some of my punctuation would not meet with the approval of a professional copy editor (someone who checks for grammar, style, punctuation and spelling).

Punctuation of direct speech can also trip you up. Should all punctuation be inside the speech marks as per the dictates of pundits such as Rene Cappon in his *Guide to Punctuation* (Associated Press, 2003), or should we follow the logical arguments of Simon Heffer in *Strictly English* (Windmill, 2010)? Take this snippet of direct speech: *Mr Smith said, "I shall have none of that nonsense in here."* Cappon would advise the terminating full stop (period) goes before the closing speech mark; Heffer would place it outside the closing speech mark: *Mr Smith said, "I shall have none of that nonsense in here".*

Who's right? (I follow Cappon's advice.) Do we care? The meaning of the sentence is clear and, in the end, if we accept that the first duty of any language, spoken or written, is to communicate meaning clearly, then either version is acceptable. I'll come back to this statement but, first, let's talk about spelling.

THE MECHANICS OF CREATIVE WRITING

Spelling

In the eighteenth century, the English writer, Samuel Johnson, sat down for nine years and, in 1755, presented his acclaimed work *A Dictionary of the English Language*, the first scholarly attempt to define the meaning of English words and their preferred spelling. His dictionary had a profound effect on all English language writers from that day forth. It unified spelling conventions and assisted the process of correct sentence construction based on the rules of grammar. As a creative writer, you will rely on your dictionary to confirm both spelling and meaning of a word but you will also observe that not everyone agrees. The American lexicographer, Noah Webster (1758 - 1843), decided he wasn't going to follow the conventional English spelling of certain words when he compiled and published *An American Dictionary of the English Language* in 1828. In a series of pre-dictionary publications, known informally as *The Blue-Backed Speller*, Webster favoured a more phonetic approach to spelling. Hence, *colour* became *color*, *defence* became *defense*, *centre* became *center*, and so on. These changes are still with us. English writers use British English spellings; American writers use American English spellings, and the differences have given rise to the aphorism *two nations divided by a common language*, variously attributed to George Bernard Shaw, Oscar Wilde, and even to Winston Churchill.

Be that as it may, as writers we tend to adhere to the spelling conventions of a particular dictionary. When in doubt, I check first with the *Concise Oxford English Dictionary*. I have a copy on my

THE MECHANICS OF CREATIVE WRITING

laptop and it's invariably left open on the desktop, ready for use. I advise you to do something similar.

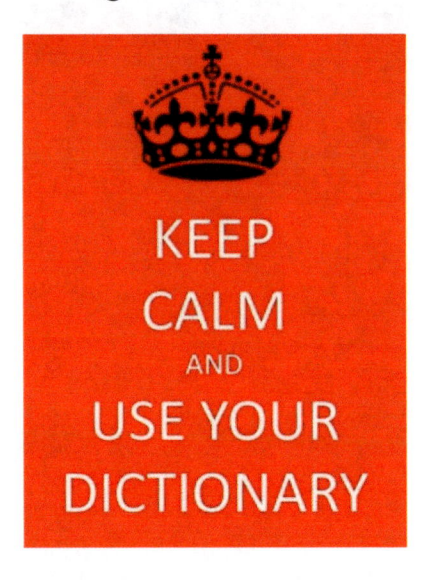

KEEP CALM AND USE YOUR DICTIONARY

I'll say more about spelling when I talk about tools later on, such as Word's built-in Spellchecker, but before I leave this topic, take a look at this.

A few years ago, an e-mail arrived in my Inbox. It contained the opening line: Eonverye taht can raed tihs rsaie yuor hnad.

Now see if you can read the following paragraph.

fi yuo cna raed tihs, yuo hvae a sgtrane mnid too. Cna yuo raed tihs? Olny 55 plepoe out of 100 can. i cdnuolt blveiee taht I cluod aulaclty uesdnatnrd waht I was rdanieg. The phaonmneal pweor of the hmuan mnid, aoccdrnig to a rscheearch at Cmabrigde Uinervtisy, it dseno't mtaetr in waht oerdr the ltteres in a wrod are, the olny iproamtnt tihng is taht the frsit and lsat ltteer be in the rghit pclae.. The rset can be a taotl mses and you can sitll raed it whotuit a pboerlm. Tihs is bcuseae the huamn mnid deos not raed ervey lteter by istlef, but the wrod as a wlohe. Azanmig huh? yaeh and I awlyas tghuhot slpeling was ipmorantt! Now I konw dfifenret.

I do not know who wrote this paragraph but it has created a lot of discussion on websites. Enter the first four words of the opening line, *Eonverye taht can raed* into a search engine and see where it takes you. (The search will miraculously suggest a corrected version of the English!) The point the author is making is that even if a word is misspelt, seriously misspelt, a reader can still determine the

18

correct word and hence make sense of the sentence using those words. That's an interesting observation but, for me as a creative writer, I would prefer to stick with conventional spellings as laid down in a dictionary and only deviate on my own terms, that is knowingly and for a purpose, rather than through ignorance and laziness. I keep in mind that, ultimately, I am writing for the enjoyment of others, my readers, and I don't want to introduce an unnecessary complication just because I can.

Rules

As I've said, there are many guidebooks on English grammar. The authors of these books set themselves up as authorities and produce erudite publications that become the basis for how we construct words from letters (spelling and meaning), how we construct sentences from words (syntax), and how we string the sentences together to form the complete literary work (sequence, paragraphing, layout and storyline). I've read many of these books (they don't always agree with each other) and, in general, I follow the consensus rules of spelling, grammar, and punctuation but I also use my own judgement. My advice to you, an aspiring creative author and writer, is choose one of the books—Gowers and Fraser, Strunk and White, Heffer, whichever takes your fancy— read it, understand it, adopt its suggestions as a base and then start writing. If you want or need to deviate, do so, but do so knowingly rather than in ignorance.

Read Around

Let me make one final suggestion to conclude this introductory chapter: read around. You probably do anyway but take a look at how other authors construct their books—the shape of their sentences, their vocabulary, layout, use of unfamiliar constructs, the presence of grammatical errors or factual errors; anything that attracts your creative eye. All these factors, and more, contribute to what is called style. Does the author have a preponderance for short sharp sentences that propel you through the narrative? How are lists of items presented—separated by commas, bullet-pointed with hyphens, numbers, or the classical filled-in small circle •, known as a flat midpoint by typographers? What about direct speech? How is the spoken word punctuated? Single or double speech marks? How about indirect speech? Just embedded or with, say, single speech marks, or in italics?

THE MECHANICS OF CREATIVE WRITING

You will find all these variations, and more, in the literary works of others and to a certain extent you will not know if a particular format is the intention of the author, the writer (if different to the author, a ghostwriter for example), the copy editor, or a style dictated by the publishing house. In a way, it doesn't matter if the meaning is clear but the key point here is to adopt a style and stick with it, at least within the confines of an individual publication. Style, a difficult term to define properly, defines an author. John le Carré has a style very different to, say, Chuck Palahniuk who, in turn, is different to, say, Cormac McCarthy. You may like one style, dislike another, and get ideas from the third but reading around will expand your literary horizons and, who knows, inspire you to develop your own, very distinct style.

(^_^)

3. The Basic Tools of Writing

Microsoft's Word Application Program

An artist who creates landscape paintings needs paint, brushes, a canvas, and an easel on which to capture the painting. A sculptor who creates ironwood carvings needs chisels, a scalpel, sandpaper, and a block of wood to convert into a thing of beauty. A composer of piano concertos needs blank sheet music paper and a piano to develop and capture the melodies. And, a writer needs something to record the grammatical constructions that will go towards building the literary creation. We need tools.

These days, the primary tool for capturing words is a word processor. I use Microsoft's word processor, Word, and, I must admit, it has made me lazy. It is so easy to correct an error that I have become what I can only describe as a *bish-bash-bosh* writer. I *bish* the words down, *bash* them around, and *bosh* them to perfection. (This is my definition of the meaning of *bish-bash-bosh*. There are other definitions.)

Another way to describe how I write is to say I smash down the words and then polish them to perfection. Now, I'm sure Charles Dickens did not bish-bash-bosh his books, nor Jane Austin. They would have taken great care in the construction of each sentence before they committed the words to paper using pen and ink.

The development of the typewriter and white correction fluid such as Tipp-Ex allowed speedier writing with on-the-fly correction of minor errors. Word processors changed all that. My own use of word processors dates back to the early 1980s when WordPerfect was launched. I loved it! I could make mistakes with impunity knowing that it was easy to go back and fix them. No more Tipp-Ex. No more I-must-get-it-right-first-time writing. Hello, creativity. Hello, laziness!

These days, I'm a power user of the ubiquitous Word program. It's perfect... well, almost perfect. I can do virtually anything I want with Word. Formatting is easy. I can change font type and size to suit. I can embed images. I can review and edit the works of others and show the corrections I've applied, plus insert pithy comments. It's a great application program and is the main tool in my writer's toolbox. And just to settle any unease you may have, I don't work for Microsoft; I've never worked for Microsoft; and Microsoft is not paying me to say these words about their product. It's just a great product and has allowed me to write and self-publish a variety of blogs and books in a way that would not have been possible pre-Word.

It's not my intention to take you through the basics of Word—there are plenty of tutorial books that do that—but I do want to draw your attention to four features that help the aspiring writer. The first is the built-in Spellchecker coupled with AutoCorrect.

Spellchecker and AutoCorrect

Word's Spellchecker is always on and can be set to the vocabulary and spellings of several languages, including English (UK) or English (US). Mine is set to English (UK) and I'm all the time educating it with the spelling of new words, alternative spellings, or words that have been omitted. It's important that you do this. The vocabulary of the English language is constantly changing.

By default, AutoCorrect is turned on when you open a new Word document. I leave it on to catch spelling errors as I type (the squiggly red line underneath a word) and to highlight a possible incorrectly structured sentence (the squiggly green line under a group of words). For me, however, the main value is its link to the built-in Spellchecker and the ability to right-mouse-click on a highlighted word to see what options I have to correct it. I pay little attention to the squiggly green line highlights. They usually prompt as a "Sentence fragment" and suggest I consider revising. Essentially, Word's grammar check looks for a subject noun and a verb and flags if one of these elements is missing. For example, "So many questions; so little time" in the summary of this book is flagged as a sentence fragment but I'm happy with the sentence as is.

AutoCorrect can be a nuisance, however. There is an option in AutoCorrect to "Automatically use suggestions from the Spellchecker". I turn this option off. I prefer to be in control of what spelling I finally use. The squiggly red line still shows, indicating a potential spelling problem, but the spelling is not autocorrected to a possibly wrong spelling that I don't spot because my eyes are on the keyboard and not on the screen.

THE MECHANICS OF CREATIVE WRITING

Styles

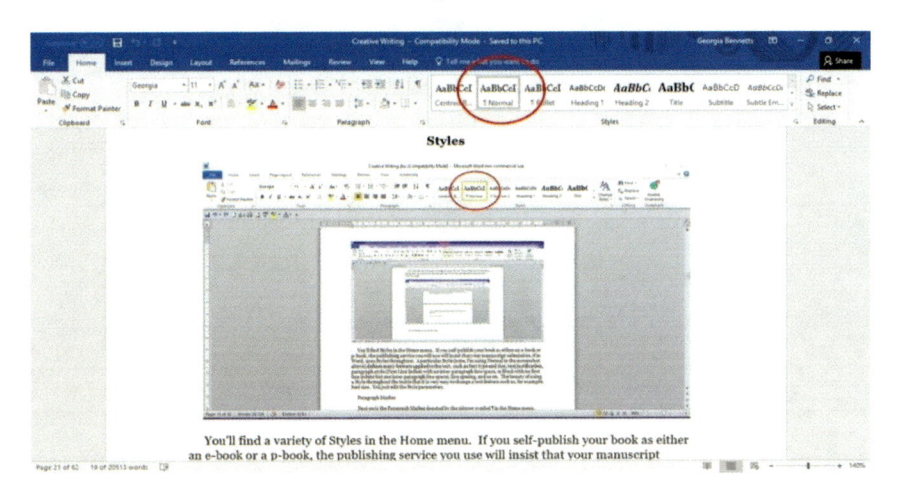

You'll find a variety of Styles in the Home menu. If you self-publish your book as either an e-book or a p-book, the publishing service you use will insist that your manuscript submission, if in Word's DOC or DOCX format, uses Styles throughout to format the text. A particular Style (note, I'm using Normal in the screenshot above) defines many attributes applied to the text, such as font type and size, text justification, paragraph style (First Line Indent with no inter-paragraph line space, or Block with no first line indent but one inter-paragraph line space), line spacing, and so on. The beauty of using a Style to control the format of the text throughout the document is that it is very easy to change a text feature such as font size or line spacing, for example. You just edit the Style parameters.

Styles are immensely powerful. You should take the time to familiarise yourself with their capabilities. It will be time well spent.

Paragraph Marker

Next is the Paragraph Marker denoted by the pilcrow symbol ¶ in the Home menu. Here you see what happens when you click on this symbol. Before:

THE MECHANICS OF CREATIVE WRITING

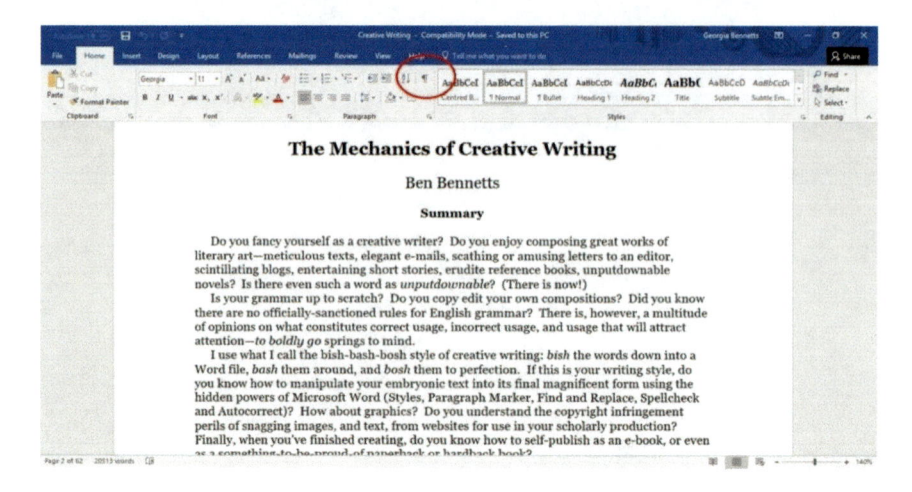

After:

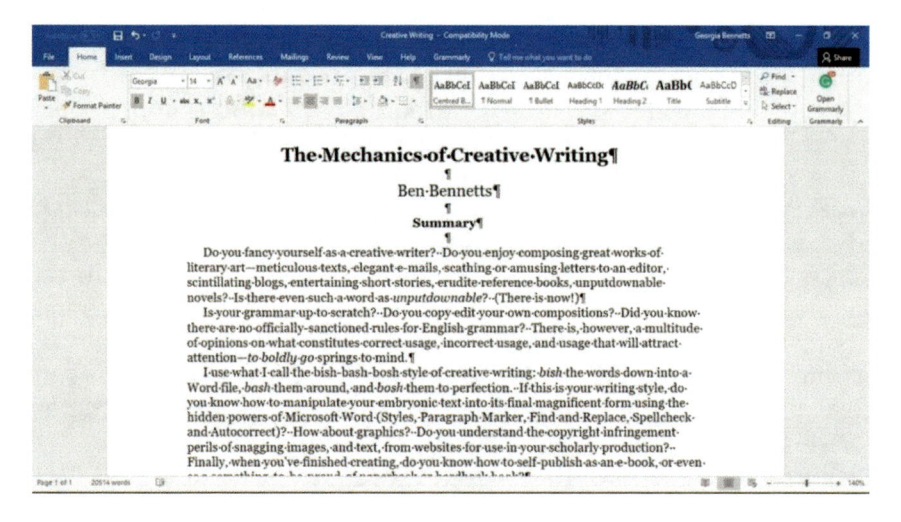

Switching the on-off Paragraph Marker on allows you to see the location of formatting marks: spaces (denoted by a small mid-line dot), paragraph mark (the ¶ symbol), tab characters, hidden text, object anchors, and optional hyphens. The Paragraph Marker feature becomes invaluable when debugging layout issues within the reflowable text of a manuscript designed to become an e-book. Play with it, see what it reveals, and use it regularly to check there are no spurious insertions in the text. It will save you a lot of debugging effort when the time comes to submit your manuscript for vetting by an e-book format checker.

Find and Replace

The fourth useful tool in Word is the powerful Find and Replace, activated either from the Find and Replace items in the Home Editing menu or, more simply, by Ctrl+F. Switching on Find enables you to search for a word or text string in the text. For example, if you are hunting to check the location of the word *only*, Find would highlight all instances of the word throughout your document. *Only Ben kissed Mary on the nose* is different to *Ben only kissed Mary on the nose* is different to *Ben kissed only Mary on the nose* is different to *Ben kissed Mary only on the nose*. Which version did you mean?

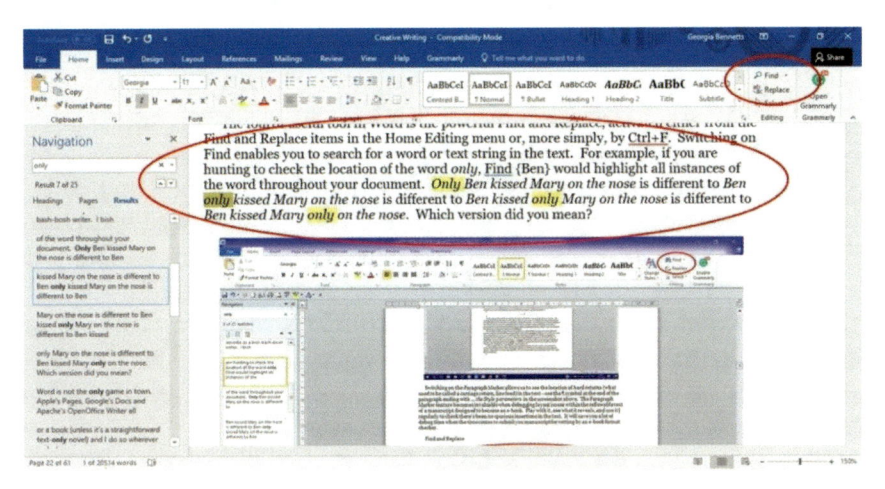

Find followed by Replace allows you to change an instance of a particular word either on a one-by-one basis or globally. If it turns out that it wasn't Ben who kissed Mary on the nose, it was Tom, then Find {Ben} and Replace {Tom} would sort it instantly.

THE MECHANICS OF CREATIVE WRITING

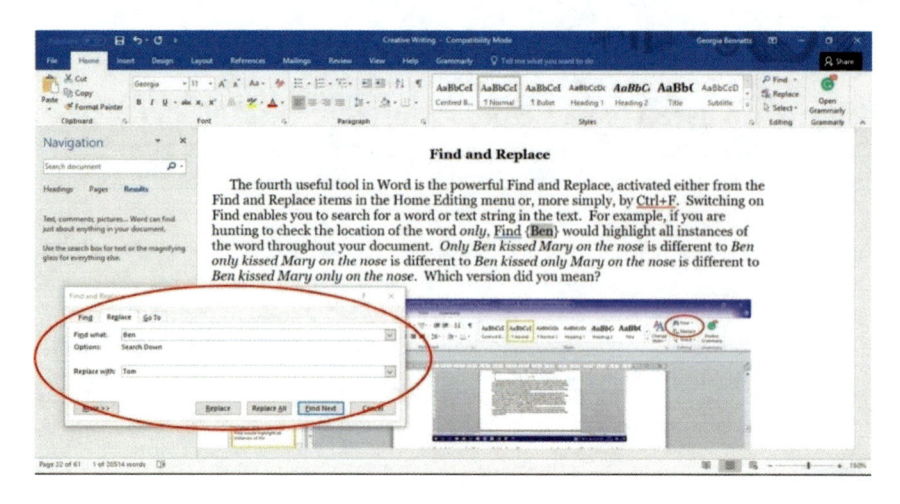

More importantly, Find and Replace protects you from yourself. The bish-bash-bosh approach to creative writing will inevitably cause many spelling errors depending on your spelling memory and finger accuracy while typing. I generate spelling errors which I either catch through Word's Spellchecker or by checking later using a dictionary, but some errors are quite devious. Take the tradename Tipp-Ex, mentioned earlier. When I first typed it, I typed it as Typex, but when I used Google to spellcheck, it threw up the correct spelling, Tipp-Ex. I corrected, added the word to Word's Spellchecker dictionary, and continued. But, I might not have made the correction instantly. I might have thought Typex was a valid spelling of the word and waited to spellcheck until I was in the polish and copy-edit phase of creating my document. I might even have used the incorrect spelling more than once. Find {Typex} and Replace {Tipp-Ex} would have resolved that problem easily.

I make heavy use of Find and Replace when editing and correcting my manuscripts. You can make the {arguments} case sensitive—Find {Tipp-ex} and Replace {Tipp-Ex}, for example. Or you can correct the spelling of a word with an acceptable alternative—Find {centre} and Replace {center}. The arguments are also space sensitive. Find { us } and replace { you } will replace *us* with *you*, whereas Find{us} and replace {you} will create some monsters, such as *becayoue, adjyoust* and *illyoutrator*! With this in mind you should be very cautious about using the global Replace All option.

Word is not the only game in town. Apple's Pages, Google's Docs and Apache's OpenOffice Writer all merit a mention. I'm not familiar with any of these alternative word processing applications but I'm sure they have similar features to those contained in Word and described above. If so, use them.

PowerPoint

In the days when I was preparing short courses on my specialist electronics subject and presenting them to classes of electronics designers and test engineers, I used Microsoft's PowerPoint presentation tool as the medium. I became conversant with the creation and manipulation of graphical images and, these days, I use PowerPoint to create some of the images I insert in my blogs and books. Most of my artworks are either screenshots, as in the images above, or a composition based on clipart, text, and inserted photographs. Here are a couple of examples taken from *The Dream Guardian*.

PICKETTY WITCH AND HER DOG, SPOT

THE MECHANICS OF CREATIVE WRITING

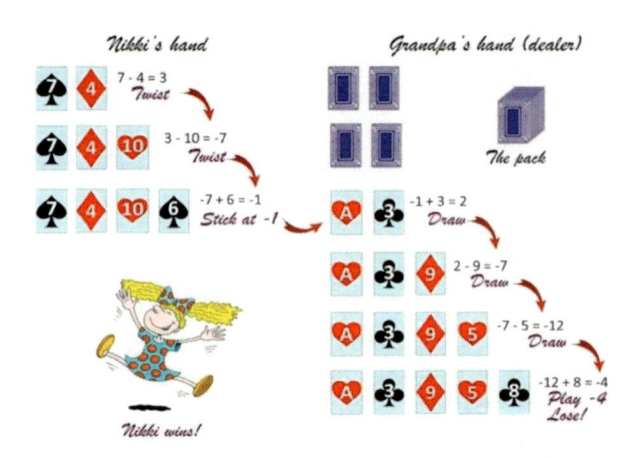

NIKKI BEATS GRANDPA AT *MAKE ZERO*

    The two examples above are not that imaginative but in the land of self-publishing you can either spend a lot of money on a professional illustrator, or find an artistic friend, or employ a do-it-yourself approach.   I think inserting images where appropriate enhance a blog or a book (unless it's a straightforward text-only novel) and I do so wherever and whenever my skills allow. The images above assume a certain familiarity with a graphics creation tool such as PowerPoint and, to be honest, images such as these are not that difficult to create. If you think adding images will enhance your manuscript, I encourage you to try PowerPoint, or one of the equivalent presentation tools such as Apple's Keynote, Google's Slides, or Apache's OpenOffice Impress.

PaintShop Pro/Photoshop

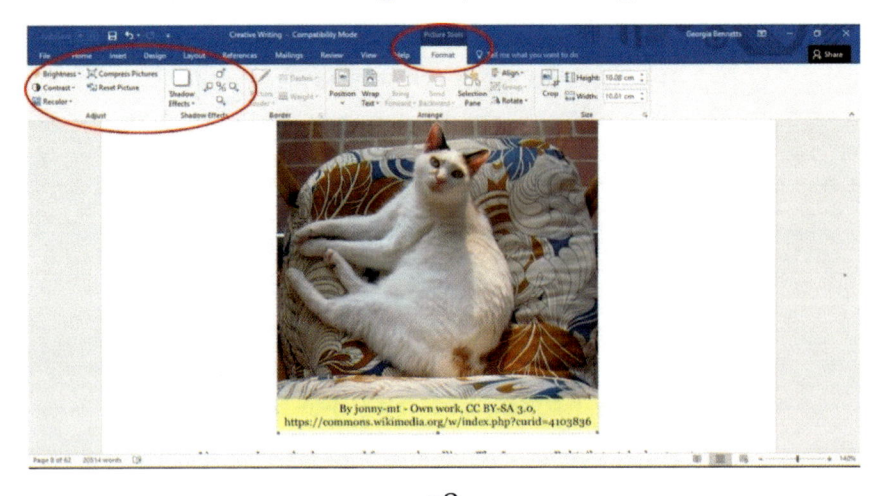

THE MECHANICS OF CREATIVE WRITING

Hand in hand with PowerPoint, you may need an image-editing program. I say may because if all you need are simple edits, such as lighten or darken, crop, sharpen or soften, adjust brightness or contrast, remove the background, and other basic image manipulations, the Adjust tools in PowerPoint's Picture Tools menu will probably suffice. But, if you need to get down and dirty with pixel manipulation, as I did in this picture from *The Dream Guardian*,

... you will need something more sophisticated. I used PaintShop Pro to insert and blend the silhouetted figure and outstretched hands with the forest. Alternatively, I could have used Photoshop.

Again, it all depends on how professional you want to be in creating images for your budding literary magnum opus. *The Dream Guardian* is a storybook for children and I wanted to show a person walking through the forest at twilight and being attacked by ghostly arms. I could find nothing that matched my requirements so I created the above image. It's not perfect but on the small screen of an e-reader it looks fine.

(^_^)

THE MECHANICS OF CREATIVE WRITING

4. Copy Edit: Polish, Polish, Polish

For every error you find and correct, you will introduce two new errors, neither of which will become apparent until your book appears in published form.
(Paraphrased from a well-known aphorism on software development.)

We come to the most important chapter in this book. You've written the first draft of your manuscript. You are proud of it but it's rough. It has come-back-to holes. It may need expansion here, reduction there. Now is the time to copy edit, to read through and start the polishing process, to add sparkle to your prose, to convert it into something someone somewhere will say, "It's a paragon of creative writing, a masterpiece, worthy of a Pulitzer or Man Booker award." But first, put it aside for a day or three. Go on a short holiday. Walk a long-distance trail. Do anything but start the polishing process. Your creation needs time to settle. The eye sees what the brain wants it to see and that's not necessarily what you have written. You need a break. I usually wait at least a day (I'm impatient!) before I start this process and I can tell you this—the polishing process will take you much longer than the initial writing phase.

Before I start, and just to be clear, let me define and differentiate between copy editing (two words when used as a verb, COED) and proofreading (one word when used as a verb, COED).

Copy Editing

Copy editing is the process of checking for grammatical mistakes, non-conformance and inconsistencies in style, punctuation errors, unnecessary repetition, fact-checking, possible copyright violations, possible libellous statements, spelling errors, and anything else that catches your eye.

The nature of most of these checks is self-explanatory. Style is the tricky one! Style is more to do with ensuring conformance to a particular convention if alternative conventions exist. For example, do we refer to a book title using speech marks—"The Dream Guardian"—or italics—*The Dream Guardian*? Both forms are acceptable but we may prefer the italics over speech marks. Similarly, do we spell copy editor as one word, two words, or two words hyphenated? You will find all three versions in the dictionaries and among the websites. You will need to select one form and stay with it. These are style issues and are part of what a copy editor checks for and corrects. The best advice I can give you about copy editing is this: find someone you know who is good at it and ask that person to copy edit your manuscript. Better still; find two or more such people. Ask family, friends, professional colleagues, anyone who's willing to take a look at your manuscript. If you copy edit your own work, which everyone does, I can guarantee you will not find all the errors. That's a 100% guarantee, a tautology I know, but I can't emphasise it enough. Don't rely only on your own skills.

Proofreading

Proofreading is different. On completion of the copy editing process, the manuscript is deemed ready for final layout prior to either printing in hard-copy form (a p-book) or displaying in soft-copy form on an e-reader screen (an e-book). Either way, the manuscript needs to be laid out appropriately. Chapter 6 details what's involved in proofreading but essentially it's to do with determining page size and margin layout, font selection and size, looking for and removing awkward end-of-line word breaks and end-of-page line breaks, insertion of bookmarks and hyperlinks (in an e-book) or page numbers and possibly an index (in a p-book), the correct placement of images vis-à-vis text, adding a table of contents, and many other items and activities associated with the final production of the book. Errors at this stage, called typographical errors, *typos* for short, are identified and fixed by a proofreader. A proofreader is not a copy editor, and vice versa, and both functions are essential to the process of publishing your book. If you perform both functions yourself, you will need all the skills to do so and these skills are not trivial. The next two chapters discuss copy editing. Chapter 6 moves on to proofreading.

THE MECHANICS OF CREATIVE WRITING

When I first started lecturing at Southampton University, I was advised that it would take ten hours to prepare a one-hour lecture. I don't know whether the *ten* is correct but the preparation time was certainly considerably longer than the presentation time. I investigated the experience of other presenters and found websites that suggested five hours instead of ten and even one speed merchant who said all he needed was two hours to prepare a one-hour presentation. I don't believe him! The actual figures don't matter, however. What matters is that usually preparation time is longer than presentation time and this is also true of manuscript reviewing and copy editing. You will spend far more time polishing your manuscript than you did writing it. When I was working on the first draft of *The Dream Guardian*, each chapter, around 3,000 words, was completed to first draft level in three to four hours, or so. But then, it took at least a further working day, sometimes longer, to polish the text and add the graphics.

The process cannot be rushed. If you are new to all this, my advice is to take it one step at a time. First, read though the draft and carry out a basic check on grammar and spelling mistakes. I call this "weeding out the sillies." Then, take a second pass paying attention to the punctuation. Then a third pass looking for and removing ambiguity in meaning. The fourth pass looks at layout (paragraphing and white space) and text formatting issues. Then, when you're done, do it all again only this time with a fine-tooth comb!

Here's a more detailed summary of this rudimentary process, taken from something I wrote in 2009 as an introduction to copy editing.

Pass 1
Always read through what you have written to check for spelling and basic grammatical mistakes. There is no excuse for bad spelling. If in doubt, use a spellchecker or a dictionary but note that spellcheckers will not correct an incorrectly spelt but valid word, *trash* instead of *thrash* for example.

Pass 2
After you've completed Pass 1, read through the text, preferably aloud, to check for and correct punctuation errors. Remember: a major role of a punctuation mark is to indicate where to breathe if you were reading the text aloud. In fact, punctuation was first developed to help actors say their lines correctly when on stage.

Pass 3
Check each sentence for clarity of meaning and remove any possible ambiguity. Ambiguity is often caused by the casual use of pronouns—*he, she, it*, and other pronoun forms. Check that every pronoun refers unambiguously to the correct predecessor noun. Be careful of *it*, especially if *it* appears at the beginning of a sentence. If in doubt, replace the pronoun with the appropriate noun. For example: *The cat sat on the rug. It was Persian.* What was Persian; the cat or the rug? Strictly speaking, it was the rug but that might not have been the intention of the writer.

Pass 4
Use paragraphing, indentation, list techniques and white space to ensure that the overall layout of the text is both supportive of the narrative and pleasing to the eye. Remember, the way you write and present your thoughts is a reflection of you as a person and an indication of your respect for the reader. Turn your writings into works of art. Unlike the spoken word, the written word can last forever as a monument to your skills as a writer and a communicator.

In addition to the simple 4-pass system, I provided a starter list of books on English grammar and the English language: Gowers and Fraser, Partridge, Truss, and Bryson, plus a dictionary and a thesaurus.

To illustrate the process, I provided an example based on an e-mail that came my way from a friend of one of my sons. Here is the original text of the e-mail.

what is she doing with these stupid web sites, I have told here she is ok with face book but this other thing is daft, we are both not smoking since jan 6th and everything going ok, no withdrawal symptons but have put a little weight on. Sorry about the leg , rest is best ,take it easy see you in the autumn

Here is my cleaned-up version of the text, changes in **bold**.

After Pass 1, Spelling and Grammar
What is she doing with these stupid **websites**, I have told **her** she is **OK** with **Facebook** but this other thing is daft, we are both not smoking since **Jan** 6th and everything **is** going **OK**, no withdrawal **symptoms** but **we** have **both** put **on** a little weight. Sorry about the leg , rest is best ,take it **easy.** **See** you in the

THE MECHANICS OF CREATIVE WRITING

autumn.

After Pass 2, Punctuation
*What is she doing with these stupid websites**?** **I** have told her she is OK with Facebook but this other thing is daft.* **We** *are both not smoking since Jan 6th and everything is going OK**: no** withdrawal symptoms**, but we have both put on a little weight. Sorry about the* **leg.** **Rest** *is* **best.** **Take** *it easy. See you in the autumn.*

After Pass 3, Ambiguity
What is **Mary** *doing with these stupid websites? I have told her she is OK with Facebook but this other thing is daft. We are both not smoking since Jan 6th and everything is going OK: no withdrawal symptoms, but we have both put on a little weight. Sorry* **to hear** *about* **your** *leg. Rest is best. Take it easy. See you in the autumn.*

The 'she' in the first sentence refers to the author's wife. I've substituted a proper noun, Mary; not her real name. I've also clarified whose leg is being talked about—the e-mail's recipient.

After Pass 4, Layout (paragraphing, white space, and other layout issues)
What is Mary doing with these stupid websites? I have told her she is OK with Facebook but this other thing is daft.

We are both not smoking since Jan 6th and everything is going OK: no withdrawal symptoms, but we have both put on a little weight.

Sorry to hear about your leg. Rest is best.
Take it easy. See you in the autumn.

That's it! This version is significantly better than the original in terms of grammar and layout. Some of the sentences would benefit from further rework but my initial 4-pass system was targeted more at correcting what already existed rather than improving the literary style. Perhaps I should add a fifth pass, Pass 5, sentence examination and reconstruction?

I wrote these words of advice in 2009, three years before I produced my first book, *The Religion Business: Cashing in on God*. Reading through them now (2018), I realise that these days I apply these checks subconsciously except I don't read aloud; I read 'in my head'. Also, I don't apply the checks just once. I will usually make three or four passes on-screen through the whole book and when I am becoming satisfied with what I see, I print out the manuscript and repeat the process. I have never yet printed out a hard copy that I haven't subsequently covered in red ink. I don't know what it is but I see all sorts of subtle errors on the sheets of paper that I do not spot on the screen. I advise you to do likewise.

Personal Style Guide

As my post-2012 writing career progressed, I started making notes about things I did wrong, spelling conventions, punctuation guidelines, and many other solecisms. I realised early on the need for consistency. Should I spell spellcheck as *spellcheck, spell check* or *spell-check*? You will find all three variations if you search the Web. The Oxford Dictionary favours *spellcheck*; Merriam-Webster opts for *spell-check*; whereas Collins offers either *spell-check* or *spell check*. As a writer, "You pays your money and takes your choice" but whichever version you plump for, be consistent within the boundaries of your book.

You can buy style guidebooks or access well-known style guides online such as the *Chicago Manual of Style* but nothing beats your own Personal Style Guide, PSG, compiled from your own experience and from reference manuals. I urge you to create your own guide and to keep it up to date.

Here's a summary of what is in my PSG as of 2018. There is no significance to the order. These are the items I've recorded as time progressed.

1. Spelling variants, -ize (American) versus -ise (British), and other American/British spelling variants.

In general, follow the -ise British-variant style for words that can end in either form.

For other spelling variants, such as *traveller/traveler, rigour/rigor, levelled/leveled, behaviour/behavior*... follow the British style.

2. Numerals and numbers
- Cardinals: one, two, three... nineteen, twenty, and then 21, 22, 23... but spell out if just one word, for example, thirty, not 30.
- Duration (adjectival use): 1-day not one-day, 30-minutes not thirty-minutes.
- Age: follow the cardinal style: twelve-year-old girl, a 27-year-old man.

THE MECHANICS OF CREATIVE WRITING

- Centuries: spell out, sixteenth century, not 16th century.
- Decades: '70s, not 70s.
- Ordinals: spell out, for example, first, second, third... not 1st, 2nd, 3rd... If ordinals are abbreviated, the style should be 12th, not 12th—that is, no superscripts.
- Dates: 27th August 2012, not 27th August 2012. Use dd/mm/yyyy order.
- Large numbers: spell out if single word, six-million Jews not 6 million Jews.

3. Quotation marks

Use double quotation marks, " ... " for quotations and direct speech (see later), and single quotation marks, ' ... ' for quotes in quotes.

4. Sentence and paragraph length

Aim for shorter rather than longer sentences and paragraphs.

5. Replacements

Replace *i.e.* with *that is*; *e.g.* with *for example* or *such as*; *etc.* with *and so on*; *whilst* with *while*; *amongst* with *among*; *WW1*, *WW2* with *World War One, World War Two*.

6. Repeated words in the same or adjacent sentences.

Use a Thesaurus to look for and replace one of the repeated words with a synonym but beware synonymitis (see later).

7. Use of contractions

Use verbal contractions sparingly to introduce a degree of chattiness to the prose but overuse detracts from the seriousness of a technical book. Be careful if using Word's Find and Replace feature to, for example, convert all instances of *I am* to *I'm*. You could finish up with "I think, therefore I'm"!

THE MECHANICS OF CREATIVE WRITING

[Photo of a dog with speech bubble: "I NEVER WIN RACES BUT I SURE LIKE BISCUITS!"]

By Hundehalter (Own work) [GFDL (http://www.gnu.org/copyleft/fdl.html) or CC-BY-SA-3.0 (http://creativecommons.org/licenses/by-sa/3.0/)], via Wikimedia Commons

8. *That* versus *which*

That introduces a defining clause (one that is essential to the overall statement). The dog *that* only has three legs never wins races.

Which introduces a commenting clause (one that is ancillary to the overall statement). The dog *which* only has three legs likes biscuits.

A person can be a *who/whom* or a *that,* but never a *which.*

A nonperson can be a *which* or a *that,* but never a *who.*

9. Text layout.

Adopt either a Block or First Line Indent paragraph formatting style. Block is preferred for technical publications. First Line Indent is preferred for narrative p-books and e-books. Don't mix the styles in the same manuscript.

10. Use of *italics*

Use sparingly but use for book titles, newspaper names, indirect speech, highlighted words.

11. Sundry grammar checks: some examples.

This is a representative sample of the sort of thing I make note of. The actual list in my PSG is much longer.

THE MECHANICS OF CREATIVE WRITING

- *Compare to* (meaning to compare similarities), *compare with* (meaning to compare similarities and differences). For example, a Seville orange can be compared *to* a Navel orange but a Seville orange compares *with* a Pink grapefruit. Shakespeare was comparing his beloved *with* a summer's day. Apparently, the beloved came out best!
- Similarly, *different from* (preferred), *different to* (okay), *different than* (use sparingly) and *comply with*, not *comply to*.
- Look for and consider removing or changing common/over-used sentence starters such as *Incidentally, Furthermore, Additionally, Accordingly, Nevertheless, Basically, Hopefully*. These words are adverbs often used to join phrases or clauses together (conjunctive adverbs). Use them sparingly to start a sentence but don't get hung up on it!
- *Reason... because; reason... why?* The reason is not *because*. The reason can be *why* but look to see if the sentence can be recast. *The reason why he took my book... -> The reason he took my book...*
- *May* (what is possible and likely to happen) and *might* (what is possible but an element of doubt exists). For example, *I may go to the party if my partner invites me whereas I might go if my boss invites me*. Assumes the partner is more favoured than the boss!
- *Practise* (verb)/*practice* (noun).
- *Programme* (a series of events, broadcast)/*program* (computer).

THE MECHANICS OF CREATIVE WRITING

THERE ARE TIMES WHEN YOU NEED AN OXFORD COMMA!

I WOULD LIKE TO THANK MY PARENTS, DONALD TRUMP AND HILLARY CLINTON.

MY MUMMY AND DADDY!

- Oxford commas rule, okay? See the illuminating example above. I suspect that the Big Prize winner meant to say, "I would like to thank my parents, Donald Trump, and Hillary Clinton." All three parties would be happy with that.
- *Backup* (adj., noun)/*back up* (verb). Example: Make sure you *back up* your Word file every hour on the hour and keep *backup* copies on an external memory such as a memory stick.
- *Hard copy/soft copy* (noun), *hard-copy/soft-copy* (adj.)
- For a.m. and p.m. time, use numbers: 4 a.m. and 6 p.m., or 4am and 6pm, or 4 am and 6 pm—pick one format and be consistent. For o'clock times, use numbers, 6 o'clock, or spell out, six o'clock (more formal), but be consistent.
- Lie, lay, lain versus Lay, laid, laid
The verb *to lie* is intransitive (requires no object) – *she lay down*. The verb *to lay* is transitive (requires an object) – *she laid a book* (object) *on the desk*.
- The position of *only* (adj., adv, conjunction) should be close to the word it modifies.
- *Between* can be between more than two things.
- *Angry with* a person; *angry at* a situation.
- Beware sexists nouns: *Chairman (Chair), Fireman (Firefighter), Policeman (Police Officer), Waitress (Server), Actress (Actor), Air Stewardess (Flight Attendant)...*
- Beware synonymitis, defined to be the process of going to great lengths to find synonyms to replace words that are oft-repeated. This may add depth and flavour but can also become distracting.

THE MECHANICS OF CREATIVE WRITING

- Check comma locations! (See Christina Sterbenz's article, Further Reading.)
- *Into* (prep.) versus *in to*? "Hold still," said Gerry, leaning in to take a closer look.
- *Any more* (two words) is reserved for the meaning *even the smallest amount*. When used as a determiner, the two-word spelling *any more* is used. "I don't want any more children."
- *Anymore* (one word) is reserved for the meaning *any longer*. When used as an adverb, the one-word spelling *anymore* is used. "You're not a little kid anymore."
- Granddaughter, not grandaughter; but grandad, not granddad.
- *Dreamed/dreamt, learned /learnt, smelled/smelt*? Use -ed versions.
- *Fewer*, things you can count, plural items. *Less*, things you can't count, singular items. I've put *fewer* eggs in this cake mix, and *less* salt.

... and many more. This list will grow continuously.

12. Passive to active voice
Prefer active. *The boy kicked the ball* is preferred over *The ball was kicked by the boy*.

13. Punctuation in direct speech
In reports and stories, a writer often wants to tell the reader what someone has said. There are two ways of doing this. The speaker's words can either be reported (in a style known as indirect or reported speech), or they can be quoted directly in what's called

direct speech. Reported speech does not use speech marks; direct speech does.

Punctuation in direct speech can get tricky. The general rule is all punctuation goes between the speech marks. For example "What's the time?" she asked. "Just gone ten o'clock," he replied.

But try this:

"Hello, Pat. How's your mother keeping these days?" Jane asked.

"Not so bad but when last I asked her, she said, 'I've still got a pain in my lower back'," replied Joan.

Here we've got direct speech within direct speech (single speech marks inside double speech marks) and a profusion of punctuation marks after the word *back*. Technically, the punctuation is correct but the sentence is better cast with the mother's reply rewritten as indirect speech inside the direct speech:

"Not so bad but when last I asked her, she said she still had a pain in her lower back," replied Joan.

~~~~~

Many of the sundry grammar checks above, especially those in Section 11, lend themselves to the Find and Replace feature in Word. You see now why I stressed this feature. It's a terrific way for finding errors, checking for spelling consistency, and reducing instances of oft-used words and phrases. For example, I have a bad habit of using *sat* when I should use *sitting*, "She was *sat* on the bed." The sentence should read, "She was *sitting* on the bed". I would never write, "She was *slept* on the bed," but in the past I have written, "She was *sat* on the bed." Strange, eh? It's clearly a grammatical blind spot. It's very easy to run a Find {*sat*} and Replace {*sitting*} check through the text to find and optionally correct this solecism (although I am now sensitised to the habit and rarely confuse *sat* with *sitting*).

I also discovered I was overly fond of starting a sentence with *However*. Not anymore. I used to oscillate between the spelling of website, one word or two? Now, it's always one. And so it goes on.

Looking at my list, you may be tempted to say that many of the items are basic grammatical howlers. I agree, and if I were to write slowly and studiously, I hope I wouldn't make them but in the heat of the initial stages of the bish-bash-bosh process, I worry not about such details. I am more concerned with the creative side; capturing the scene, laying down the basic dialogue, setting out the action, telling the story. Hence, I make mistakes necessitating the polishing stage. As I said earlier, word processing application programs make you lazy but also offer you tools to find and correct your errors.

THE MECHANICS OF CREATIVE WRITING

I make heavy use of my Personal Style Guide, not only for blogs and books but even for e-mails. I am continuously adding to the checklists, especially section 11, and I recommend you follow suit if, like me, you favour the bish-bash-bosh style of creative writing.

Use of Online Grammar Checkers

You will find several online grammar checkers: Grammarly, GrammarCheck, Scribens, Ginger, and so on. Word has a built-in grammar checker which is not very tolerant of anything out of the box—no subject noun, for example (identified as a fragment), or unusual punctuation. I do look at Word's suggestions but most times I reject them.

Grammarly (slogan: Write ~~Gooder~~ Better with Grammarly) offers a basic grammar-checking service for free plus an advanced service in return for a subscription. I registered for the free service and installed the Grammarly add-in for Word. The tool is easy to use and offers advice in several areas: spelling (including the use and abuse of hyphens), punctuation, verb tense and noun matching, British English versus American English (spelling and style), and several others types of checks. But, and it's a big but, your knowledge of English grammar needs to be at least reasonable before you start using and responding to Grammarly's suggestions. Grammarly will not teach you about English grammar but does offer an explanation for an alleged error. Grammarly will help you find errors you either missed or were not aware of when you carried out your pre-Grammarly check. Here are just a few examples taken from the first draft of a new book written by a friend of mine and sent to me with a request to copy edit.

Spelling suggestions

Original text: ... *at an infant's school in her home town of Millhaven*.
Grammarly's suggestion: change *home town* to *hometown*.
Comment: Agreed. *Hometown* is one word, not two. *Infant's school* missed.

Original text: ... *and the children at the infants school where she worked were*...
Grammarly's suggestion: change *infants* to *infant's*.
Comment: Just one infant? The usual way of describing a school for infants is *infant school*, not *infants' school* or *infant's school*.

THE MECHANICS OF CREATIVE WRITING

Punctuation suggestions

Original text: *"It's from Dorothy" she said.*
Grammarly's suggestion: insert a comma after *Dorothy*.
Comment: Agreed.

Original text: *"You're home early love."*
Grammarly's suggestion: insert a comma after *home*.
Comment: An incorrect suggestion. Place a comma after *early*.

Noun Verb Mismatch

Original text: *A green and blue checked rug was slung over his shoulder.*
Grammarly's suggestion: change *was* to *were*.
Comment: Blatantly incorrect. There's only one rug.

Original text: *There was a new brightness and determination about her countenance.*
Grammarly's suggestion: change *was* to *were*.
Comment: No, no, no!

British English versus American English
Note: Grammarly offers two dictionaries—British English and American English. I selected British English.

Original text: *Mr. Neville Chamberlain's voice...*
Grammarly's suggestion: change *Mr.* to *Mr*
Comment: Agreed. American English places a full stop after an abbreviated title. British English doesn't.

Other checks

Original text: *... and often talked of their plans for the future.*
Grammarly's suggestion: change *talked of* to *talked about*.
Comment: Preposition change. Debatable. *Talked of* is in common usage.

Original text: *One of her plaits had come undone...*
Grammarly's suggestion: Confused word: change *plaits* to *plants*.
Comment: Not agreed. It was definitely a plait that had come undone.

THE MECHANICS OF CREATIVE WRITING

Original text: ... *had been told by the Ministry for War that...*
Grammarly's suggestion: change *Ministry for* to *Ministry of*.
Comment: Well spotted by Grammarly. The UK Ministry was named the Ministry *of* War.

Original text: ... *would also be devastated with this news.*
Grammarly's suggestion: Confused preposition: change *devastated with* to *devastated by*.
Comment: Subtle, but a correct suggestion.

Original text: *Back in her bedroom, as she began dressing herself for her wedding, Amy...*
Grammarly's suggestion: Redundant reflexive pronoun: *herself.*
Comment: Agreed. I deleted *herself.*

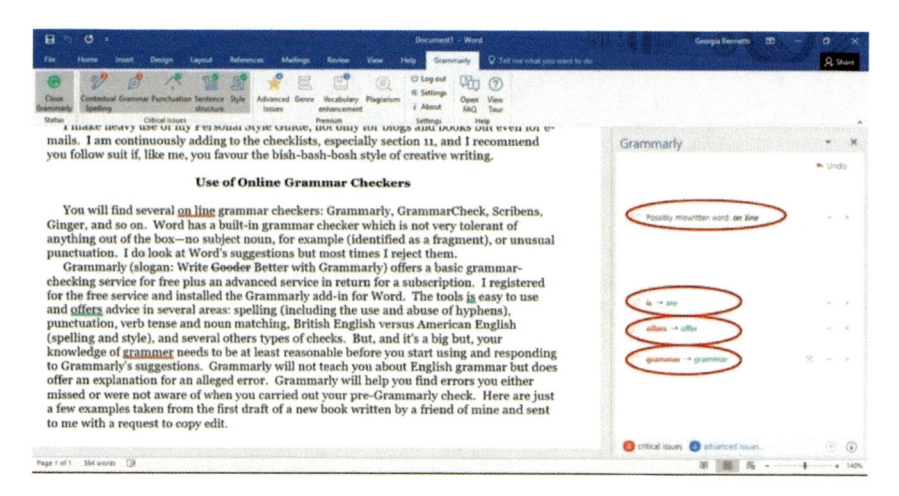

I applied Grammarly to one of my books, already published (just under 88,000 words). Grammarly flagged up 854 critical issues and 1,381 advanced issues. Gulp! The advanced issues are only visible if you pay to use the service. The critical issues are shown alongside the document (see illustrative screenshot above), and I worked my way through them. Some issues were indeed errors on my part. Some were clearly not errors at all. And some issues were debatable. Here's a sample of the more interesting suggestions Grammarly found in my book:

Original text: *None of the reports go into the detail...*
Grammarly's suggestion: change *go* to *goes*.

44

THE MECHANICS OF CREATIVE WRITING

Comment: This suggestion assumes *none* is singular. *None* can also be plural in construction but I accepted the change.

Original text: *Then the three of us were placed around a small table...*
Grammarly's suggestion: change *around* to *on*.
Comment: No. We were placed *around* the table, not *on* the table!

Original text: *If so, you have become a smartphonolic (noun: a person addicted to their smartphone) and...*
Grammarly's suggestion: change *smartphonolic* to *smart phenolic*.
Comment: *Smartphonolic* is my neologised invention. I've added the word to my personal dictionary in Grammarly.

Original text: *... to the real world populated with real people.*
Grammarly's suggestion: change *populated with* to *populated by*.
Comment: Agreed.

Original text: *She's too busy chasing down illusive Pokémon Go creatures.*
Grammarly's suggestion: change *illusive* to *elusive*.
Comment: A homophonic error; a bad mistake on my part! The two words are quite different in meaning.

Original text: *... to "prove" that each of these entities are zero.*
Grammarly's suggestion: change *are* to *is*.
Comment: mea culpa!

Original text: *There are no officially-sanctioned rules but there are a multitude of opinions on what constitutes correct usage...*
Grammarly's suggestion: change the second *are* to *is... but there is a multitude of opinions...*
Comment: We could argue all night on this one. Is *multitude* singular (the collective opinions) or plural (the individual opinions)? I probably meant the latter and accepted the suggested correction. After all, I would write *There is a herd of cows on the hillside*, not *There are a...*

Original text: *But, I draw the line at saying "Bill and me went to the shops".*
Grammarly's suggestion: change *me* to *I*.

THE MECHANICS OF CREATIVE WRITING

Comment: Precisely! But comma after *saying* was missed.

Of the 854 critical issues, I responded positively to at least 100, maybe more, and learned a very valuable lesson: I am fallible! Many of my mistakes were double-worded spelling mistakes—two words or one, with or without a hyphen—and possible punctuation errors but punctuation is always a bit iffy. Would you add a comma after *First* in this sentence: *First we open the book so that we can browse its contents?* Would you delete the colon after *are* in this sentence: *Examples of popular search engines are: Google, Yahoo, Bing, Ask.com, and so on?* The answers depend on how you would say each sentence aloud, with or without a slight pause after *First;* with or without a major pause after *are*.

There were many other 'errors' I chose to ignore: suggestions I had used the wrong word (*fire* to replace *ire*, *plants* to replace *plaits*, *started* to replace *startled*...); style issues (*9 March 2017* instead of *9 March, 2017*); and some very interesting suggestions for some French words I had used in one particular section of the book. But, overall, I gained a lot by subjecting my book to Grammarly and my conclusion is that the check is a useful adjunct to your own skills as a copy editor but requires you to have a good working knowledge of grammar in order to decide what to accept and what to ignore. If you blindly accept all Grammarly's suggestions, you will finish up with gobbledegook!

After my trial runs with Grammarly, I contemplated buying the professional version but so far have not done so. Try this short quiz. Can you explain the following grammatical terms?

- dangling modifier;
- gerund versus participle;
- passive versus active voice;
- squinting modifier;
- comma splice;
- appositives;
- superlative versus comparative.

Do you believe that splitting the infinitive is wrong? How about starting a sentence with a conjunction and ending with a preposition? Is this something up with which you will not put? Was the girl *sat* in the chair or *sitting* in the chair, or don't you care? Is *I'd* a contraction for *I had* or *I would* or should *I'd* be avoided as a contraction?

My point is, if you know the answers to these questions, you've no need to upgrade to the professional version of Grammarly because you will not commit solecisms of these types or, if you do, you will do so deliberately. If you don't know the answers, what will you do with Grammarly's suggestions?

Okay, okay, it's not as simple as this but you will need a reasonable knowledge of English grammar to make sense of Grammarly's advice and if you have this knowledge why do you need the advice? Also, if you have this knowledge, you will almost certainly 'break the rules' in the interest of creative writing. As I've already said, there is no definitive set of English-grammar rules maintained by an official organisation so who is to pronounce what is right and wrong? When Woody Harrelson said, "You ain't seen nothin' yet," in the movie *Natural Born Killers*, it seemed he was committing a grammatical crime of magnificent proportions but there was no mistaking what he meant! And, in any case, if he had said, "You have seen somethin' yet," (the logical result of cancelling the two negatives), his statement would have made no sense and carried no threat.

One of the beauties of writing in the English language is that the lack of firm rules allows creative writing to flourish. Grammarly runs the risk of stifling this freedom. How do you think Shakespeare would have reacted to Grammarly's advice had he submitted his manuscripts for scrutiny before publication?

Use the professional version of Grammarly with caution. Use the free version to catch stupid errors but be prepared to question and reject many of the suggestions.

Footnote. I ran an early draft of the text of this book through Grammarly. It found 306 so-called critical errors which is not surprising given all the deliberate misspellings throughout the book, but 84 'errors' were of interest. Most were unintentional misspellings but a few merited further investigation and resulted in changes to the text.

Fact-check

One final comment about the polishing process. Make sure you fact-check. (I accept there is now a verb *to fact-check*. Soon, it will be written *to factcheck* or even *facheck*!)) Before you misguidedly state that George Orwell published his *Nineteen Eighty-Four* book in 1984, check it out. (The year was 1949.) If you quote someone's year of birth or death, check it out. If you reference a book and want to include details such as the publisher and year of publication, check it out. And, don't always rely just on Wikipedia. I am a heavy user of Wikipedia (I even donate money now and again) but, in some cases, I look elsewhere either to confirm Wiki's statements or, maybe, to get a different perspective. I did this when I researched my book on religion. Wiki had good basic articles on the world's major religions but I found informative supplementary content on other websites.

THE MECHANICS OF CREATIVE WRITING

Fact-checking is important. Be diligent in your searches. Don't let your book be cited for presenting incorrect facts. Your reputation will suffer.

(^_^)

5. Copyright: the Perils of Copy and Paste

It's all too easy these days to copy a piece of text or an image from a website and paste it into your document but, if you do so, be aware of copyright laws. I first came up against this issue when I wrote my book on religion in 2011-2012 and wanted to quote from books and websites and make use of website images. The onus was on me to make sure I was not infringing anyone's copyright and I researched the topic and wrote a summary of my understanding. Here is an updated version of that summary.

Copyright, and How to Avoid Copyright Infringement Lawsuits

> Using and then quoting full details of the source of a text extract or graphical image is not a legal substitute for obtaining permission from the copyright holder.

1. Disclaimer

The following summary of Copyright Law and how it applies to public and private publications is based on my own interpretation of the laws. It is not a definitive set of rules and you use the advice at your own risk. Copyright law is notorious for being vague and ambiguous and, if in doubt, you are advised to seek proper advice from a Copyright Lawyer. I am not a Copyright Lawyer.

2. Introduction

In the course of producing the first draft of my 2012 book on religion, I made use of extracts of text and graphics (images) copied from websites, quotations ascribed to well-known people or authors, and e-mails I had received. When the first draft of my book was finished, I investigated copyright law to assess it for any possible infringements. Here is my admittedly layman's understanding of copyright law as it applies to text and graphics, quotations, and e-mails.

3. Definitions

Copyright is the intrinsic and automatic legal right of the creator of something deemed to be original (something involving a degree of creative skill, judgement and workmanship) to control the use of his or her creation by any third party. Copyright applies to works in literature, graphic imagery, music, works of art, audio, film, and drama.

A **public-domain** publication is any written communication available to a member of the public either for money, barter, or as a gift. For a book, a public domain offering will usually have an International Standard Book Number, ISBN, assigned to it and may be available through any number of walk-in or online bookshops or other commercial outlets.

A **private edition** of a publication is one where the author or his or her representative creates copies of the publication, usually a limited number, and puts a strict control on their distribution. The publication may be intended only for family and friends and is neither available to nor intended for any member of the general public. It is usually classed as not-for-profit and it may contain a statement inside the book that identifies its private status—see later.

Text is any extract of written material from a website or publication, in any language and ascribed to the originator of the website content or to the publication.

Graphic is any line drawing, artwork (illustration, figure, diagram, clipart), logo, map, photograph, table, or chart and similarly ascribed to the originator.

4. Application of Copyright Law to copyrighted text or graphics used in a public domain publication

The default position is that any text, image or e-mail copied from a website or copied from another publication, with or without the presence of the © symbol and legend, is subject to copyright protection unless otherwise stated and should always be attributed to the originator. (Note: the textual content of e-mails is considered in exactly the same way as text obtained from websites and books.) This means that you should *always* seek and obtain permission from the originator before use unless there is a clear statement saying that the item has been placed in the public domain and can be used freely in any further publication. But, there are exceptions under what is known as *fair use,* also known as *fair dealings,* usage.

These exceptions are for use of copyrighted text and graphics used in publications for private research, educational purposes, the reporting of news, and lending by libraries.

Fair use also applies to extracts used in commercial for-profit public domain offerings but if in doubt, seek permission rather than assume that permission is not required. See next section.

Beware paraphrasing to overcome a potential copyright infringement and beware the temptation to modify the original text, even if it's only a minor grammatical correction.

4.1 Application of *fair use* to text extracted from websites or books

Specifically, for text extracted from websites or books and used in a commercial public offering, some publishers suggest that *fair use* is applicable to text containing less than 1,000 words. Others suggest less than 100 words. In both cases, the limits apply to the accumulation of all quotations from a single source, not just to each individual quotation.

The Society of Authors and The Publishers Association, two separate organisations, have, in the past, suggested the following guidelines for when to seek permission to use copyrighted text:
- If a single extract is greater than 400 words.
- If a series of extracts from the same source totals more than 800 words.
- If any extract totals more than 25% of the original publication.

But note these limits are only guidelines, not legal rules. In the end, each case is judged on its merit and based more on quality (what does the extract add to the publication?) than on quantity (word count).

In subjective terms, *fair use* is intended to cover short quotations from well-known authors or celebrities, and short text extracts. The fun starts when you try to define what is meant by 'short'.

THE MECHANICS OF CREATIVE WRITING

There is also the 70-year rule that states that text created more than 70 years after the death of the originator, or if the originator is unknown, 70 years after the work was created, is no longer subject to copyright protection. Thus quotations from the Bible or the Qur'an do not require the permission of the original authors. Thank God for that!

4.2 Application of *fair use* to graphics in public domain publications

Here the advice is simple: *always* obtain permission before using any graphical images in a public domain publication unless the clipart website states that their clipart is royalty free and may be used as long as the source is attributed, such as Wikimedia Commons, Flickr and OpenClipart. This even applies, for example, to clipart taken from Microsoft's ubiquitous Clipart Library. Clipart from this library is freely available and can be used for both commercial and non-commercial usage as long as the source is attributed. What you can't do with Microsoft's clipart is re-package a media element and sell it on to a third party. But use in a book such as this is fine.

There is no *fair use* application to graphical images. If you are not able to obtain permission for a copyrighted royalty-loaded graphical image, either delete the image from your publication or create your own version of the image in a way that does not attract accusations of plagiarism (the use of someone else's copyrighted material without assigning due credit).

Note also that any photograph you use that contains a recognizable face requires a signed Model Release Form from the person depicted. The form grants the photographer the right to make the image and then make use of the image in any way he or she sees fit—*transmit the image in any medium and for any purpose throughout the world.*

In general, assessment of *fair use* is influenced by the purpose of the use (to increase the commercial value of your publication, for example), the nature of the use (ridicule or praise, for example), and the amount of the text extract or number of graphics relative to the size of your publication. The assessment may also be influenced by whether you have any money or other material assets and therefore become a potential target for a lawsuit!

5. Application of Copyright Law to text or graphics used in a private edition of a publication

Here, there seem to be no rules. A publication intended for distribution to a private audience as described in section 3 can contain anything you want and does not require permission from the originators. You are advised to insert words to this effect inside the book; something along these lines:

> **Copyright Law Disclaimer**
>
> This book is published as a private publication, distributed by the author and is not meant to be sold, given away, or in any other form made available in the public domain. There may be copyright issues with some of the content. I will either resolve these issues or withdraw the content before publishing a public domain version of the book.

6. Obtaining permission

To obtain permission to use text or graphics in your book, you need first to find the owner of the copyright—the originator. This may not be easy! In the course of trying to obtain permission to use copyrighted text and graphics in my 2012 book, I experienced responses ranging from no response (very common) to, "I've no idea who owns the copyright; I just use it," to "Good question; I'll get back to you," (they never do). Rarely did I get an answer that admitted ownership and granted free use of the text or image. It was, and still is, a jungle!

In the case of text quoted from a book, look at the Copyright Notice inside the book and approach the publisher first. In the case of graphics or text on a website, approach the webmaster or, if known, the originator via e-mail or a Contact form on the website. An approach by e-mail is acceptable, as is an e-mailed reply, but in all cases ensure that there is some form of written record rather than, say, a telephone call.

You should include the following in your permission request:
- Details of the text extract, graphic, quotation or e-mail, including the source (website with date, book, other), and with any changes you propose to make to the original.
- Confirmation that he or she owns the copyright.
- Ask for the Terms and Conditions of the permission. It may be given freely or in return for a fee.
- The originator's Credit Line (how he or she wants to be acknowledged).
- Details of your intended use of the copyrighted material.

If you do not receive a reply after the initial request followed by multiple chasers and you decide to go ahead and include the item, you should put a note in the book inviting copyright owners to contact you for restitution if they feel that their copyright has been breached. This is not a protection against a potential infringement lawsuit but it shows you tried to obtain permission and are willing to apply retrospective restitution.

Good luck!

7. A Typical UK Copyright Clause

Copyright © 2017, Ben Bennetts

All rights reserved. No part of this publication may be reproduced or transmitted in any form or by any means, electronic or mechanical including photocopying, recording or any information storage or retrieval system, without prior written permission in writing from the publishers.

The right of Ben Bennetts to be identified as the author and illustrator of this work has been asserted by him in accordance with the Copyright, Designs and Patents Act 1988.

Every effort has been made to trace all copyright holders of material, textual and graphic, quoted or otherwise used in this book. Any omissions will be acknowledged and included in future editions if application is made in writing or by e-mail to the author at ben@ben-bennetts.com .

First published in the United Kingdom in 2017 by Atheos Books.

ISBN-13: 978-1546989585
ISBN-10: 1546989587

(^_^)

6. Publishing your Book: E-book or P-book?

You're done. You've polished your manuscript so many times you are beginning to hate the sight of it. That's natural. Take another break of a few days or more, and then return to polish it one more time. I find that no matter how many times I've worked my way through a manuscript, I always, always, find something new every time I read it. This is not such a problem when you publish as an e-book because you can upload a corrected version of the file onto the online bookseller's website, but it's a major pain if you've published as a p-book. When the first edition of *The Dream Guardian* came out as a p-book, one of my granddaughters read the book and pointed out that in the sentence, *"Insects eat leaves, mice eat insects, eagles eat mice, but who eats the eagle?" Grandpa mused,* it was Arthur who mused, not Grandpa. Aargh! I kicked myself. I went off and sulked. Then I took it on the chin and vowed to do better next time!

I carry out all the initial copy editing tasks required by a new manuscript and there is always the danger I won't catch all the errors. I accept this but I work hard to eliminate as many errors as possible. If you can find someone else to at least check for basic errors such as my Grandpa/Arthur mistake, cajole or pay them to do it. I lean heavily on family and friends and always they find additional faults. That may be a reflection of my skills or it may be that, as the author, I see what I want to see rather than what I have written. Another reason is that different people have different strengths and weaknesses, so that getting others to review my work will almost always show up things I've missed.

Incidentally, when you copy edit your own work, you will edit the master file. If someone else offers to copy edit your manuscript, you have two choices: either send them a hard copy for them to read, mark up and return, or send the master DOC file and ask them to use Track Changes and New Comment in Word's Review menu. The former may be easier for the reviewer whereas the latter may be easier for you.

At some point, you will say enough is enough and decide to self-publish your new book. The first decision is e-book or p-book, or both? Let's examine the pros and cons.

Publishing as an E-book

Of the two publishing options, publishing as an e-book is easier. I publish with two major online e-book distributors: Smashwords and Amazon's Kindle Direct Publishing, KDP. Both websites will take you gently through the submission procedure and both will offer advice on how to format the original Word file for e-book publication. Here's what you need to know.

Forget page by page boundaries. There are no page numbers in an e-book. The text is reflowable. This means it is considered to be one long continuous page and, based on the font size chosen by the reader, will display one screen full at a time. Hence, there is no requirement to insert a title or chapter header or a page number footer.

You should also avoid footnotes. If you want to add ancillary detail, either find a way to insert it within the main text or use bookmarked endnotes and hyperlink to the endnote from within the main text. If you adopt this technique, don't forget to include a link back to the text at the end of the endnote.

If your book is technical or in some other way a reference book and you are tempted to use Word's Mark Entry/Insert Index features to create an index, don't! Each entry will show as an indexed term at the end of the book, or wherever you choose to place the completed index, but given that there is no concept of a page number in the reflowable text, your index will look like a long series of single-entry endnotes. The reader will find the entry and if there's only one main text reference, jump to it via the hyperlink. If there are multiple entries, the reader will have to keep returning to the indexed item and then travel back to each reference. So what, you ask? That's what happens with multiple references in the index of a printed book. Yes, it is, and it is possible to create a similar index in an e-book but navigating back and forth through the reflowable text is not as easy as in a printed book. But, if your book requires it, do it.

THE MECHANICS OF CREATIVE WRITING

On websites such as Smashwords and Kindle Direct Publishing, you will be asked to submit a Word file, either DOC (Smashwords) or DOCX (KDP), and your file will first be checked for formatting errors (I'll come back on this in a minute) and then converted into the two most common e-book reader formats, EPUB and MOBI. Your file may also be converted into an Adobe PDF but a PDF file is not a reflowable text file. The PDF will be a standard page size and with no option for the reader to change the font size.

A MOBI file is the format used by Amazon on their Kindle tablets. EPUB is a file format standard published by the International Digital Publishing Forum and is the most widely supported format with EPUB readers on just about every other e-reader tablet. Having said this, there are EPUB reader apps that can be installed on a Kindle to allow a Kindle user to read an EPUB file, and similarly, you can find a MOBI reader to install on, say, an iPad to enable an iPad user to read a MOBI file. The bottom line is that you will need to convert your DOC or DOCX file to both target e-reader formats.

Conversion is usually straightforward and carried out automatically by converters on the online bookstore websites but you will need to make sure your file is properly formatted before submission. Here are some of the things to take care off. The following summary relates more to the requirements of Smashwords but the rules for KDP are almost identical.

Before we get to the specifics, note that your DOC/DOCX file must be clean to start with. This means stripped of any hidden clutter inserted by Word when you created the original file. Clutter, defined to be unwanted formatting marks or corrupted styling, can occur if you have played around with Styles, text fonts, index entries, bookmarks, WordArt, headers, footers, tabs, tables, text boxes, and so on, or if you have imported your file from another word processor. If you suspect your file contains clutter, Smashwords recommends the nuclear method for cleaning: cut and paste everything into Notepad, save, and then cut and paste everything back from Notepad into a new Word file and save as a DOC file. This will strip out all formatting. Now reformat the new Word file using Styles.

Formatting Dos and Don'ts for an E-book

Here is a short list of things I do when preparing a file for submission to Smashwords.

THE MECHANICS OF CREATIVE WRITING

Formatting Text

● Show spaces, line feeds and other hidden formatting using Word's Show/Hide ¶ (pilcrow) in Paragraph. This will reveal unwanted spaces and line throws. Delete them.
● Cosmetic white space is best kept to a minimum. Insert one, or two at the most, hard returns between text. MOBI/EPUB converters don't like unnecessary white space and will remove it.
● Don't insert page numbers, or any other form of a header or footer.
● Use Page Breaks sparingly, for example, only at the end of a chapter.

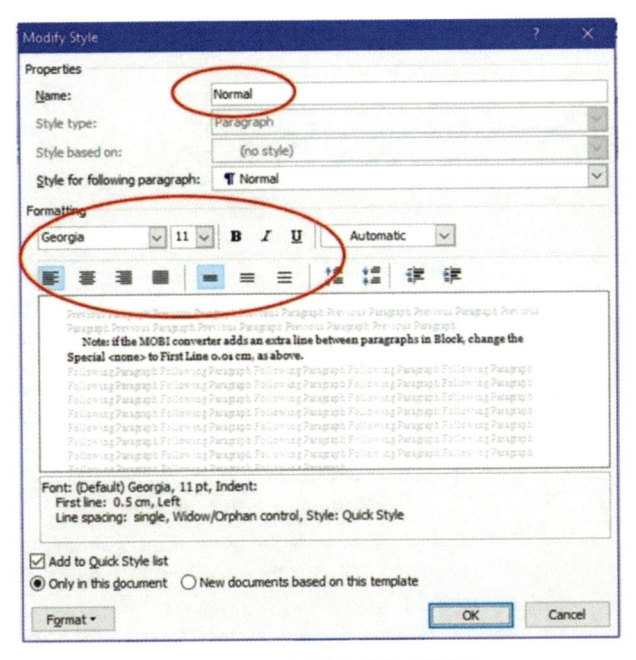

NORMAL STYLE FOR TEXT

● Set text line spacing to single space, left justified, 11 or 12 point font size. Use the Normal Style as above.

THE MECHANICS OF CREATIVE WRITING

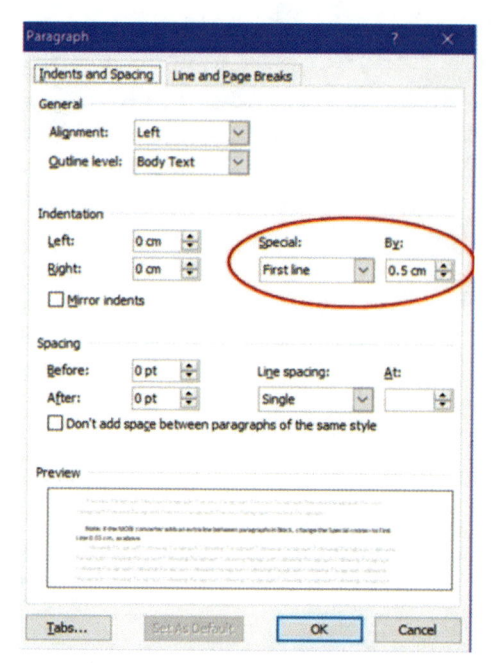

FIRST LINE INDENT PARAGRAPH STYLE

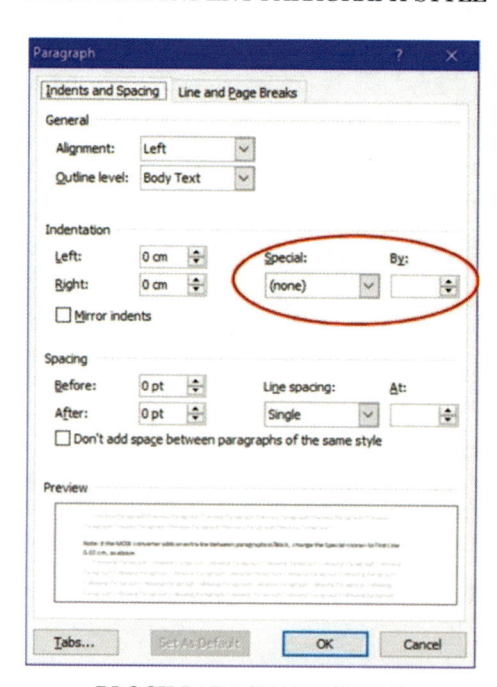

BLOCK PARAGRAPH STYLE

- Paragraph Styles. Use Styles to define the paragraph formatting styles First Line Indent (preferred for p-books and e-books) and Block (preferred for technical publications and favoured by bloggers).
- Never use the tab or space bar keys to create first-line indents or other deliberate white space. Always use a Style.
- Similarly, don't use the Centre button in the Paragraph menu to centre images, text and headings. Use a Centred Style based on Normal.
- Don't use Word's Bullets feature in Paragraph to insert a bullet or numbering symbol in a list of items. The Bullets feature in Paragraph uses tabs, and format converters currently remove the tab indentations thus modifying the display of your list. Create a Bullet Style based on Normal that indents the text to, say, 0.5 cm, and then use Insert Symbol to insert a leading bullet symbol per item. Note: this list, and all other lists in this book, are styled in this way.
- Avoid fancy fonts. Stick to Arial, Times New Roman, Georgia or Garamond at 11 or 12 font size, 14 max. A popular combination is size 12 for text and size 14 for centred headings.
- Don't use different font colours. Stay with black and set as Automatic in Font Colour.
- If you insert special marks such as ê, é, ä, ï, €, ©, ®, §, check the marks display correctly in the EPUB and MOBI conversions. Text formatting such as **BOLD**, *Italics*, <u>Underline</u>, ~~Strikethrough~~, ^{superscripts} and $_{subscripts}$ are permissible.
- Don't insert text boxes or tables, or reformat text into multiple columns. Current format converters cannot handle these formatting features.
- Don't insert footnotes. Use endnotes (sparingly) and Bookmark/Hyperlink to navigate the text.
- Keep chapter titles short and create a Table of Contents, TOC, using Bookmark/Hyperlink. Don't use Word's automatic TOC feature. Remove all hidden bookmarks: Insert -> Bookmark and then click on Hidden Bookmarks (identified with a leading _Hltxxx... name).

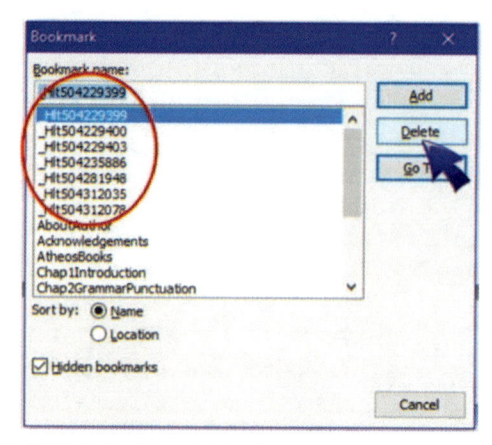

FINDING AND REMOVING HIDDEN BOOKMARKS

• Call chapters Chapters, not Part, Section or any other variation. (This assists automatic Navigation panel creation by the converter.)

Note: format converters are improving all the time and many of these restrictions may not apply anymore.

Formatting and Inserting Images

• Format your embedded image as a PNG or JPEG. Use PaintShop Pro or Photoshop to resize to 150 dpi (max), width 5 cm (minimum), 8 cm (normal), or 15 cm (max). Use References -> Insert Caption to add a centre-locked caption, or insert centred text immediately below the image.
• To ensure an image appears correctly on an e-reader page, use a Centred Style and do not insert any text either side of an image.
• If the converter complains about image size, use Word's Compress feature to compress images either down to Web/Screen resolution of 96 dpi or, if the converter will allow, Print resolution of 200 dpi. To use Compress, select an image and double-click to bring up the Picture Tools Format options.

THE MECHANICS OF CREATIVE WRITING

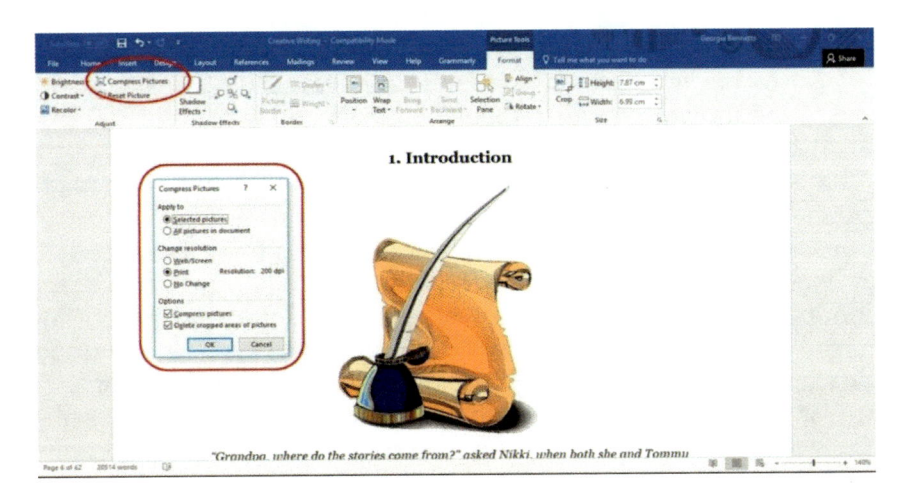

- Create a front cover: JPEG or PNG, 1,600 pixels x 2,400 pixels (at least), 200 dpi or better, rectangular portrait with aspect ratio between 1.5 and 1.6, RGB not CMYK colour scheme.

A Final Check using Calibre

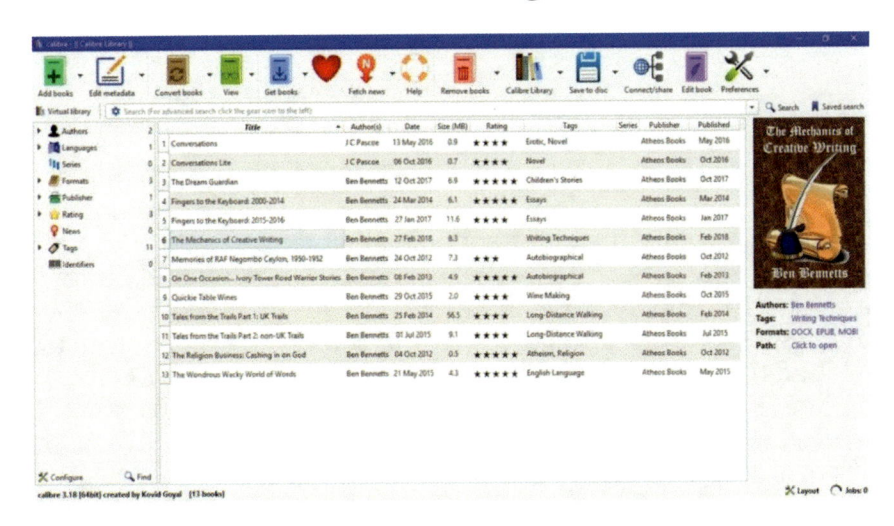

Before you submit your manuscript to either Smashwords or Kindle Direct Publishing, take a first look at the MOBI and EPUB versions of your e-book using a free e-book manager called Calibre (download details in the Online Publishing and Printing Services section in Further Reading at the end of the book). Calibre allows you to convert, manage and view your collection of e-books. I use it to convert my final manuscript (note: submitted in DOCX, not DOC format) into both an EPUB and a MOBI format which I then view to check for layout issues such as spurious bookmarks, off-centre images, and unwanted white space.

That's it! The first time through the process will cause you to go back and edit, yet again, your manuscript but subsequent submissions will be easier. I found Smashwords to be a relatively easy experience once I had downloaded, digested and applied the guidelines presented in Mark Coker's *The Smashwords Style Guide*. Amazon's KDP offers similar guidelines and both services are free and take you smoothly through the process of converting your manuscript into an e-book and then offering it to anyone who finds it and wants to buy it. Note: Smashwords allows you to offer your book as a free download if that's what you want to do. KDP does not. KDP insists on a minimum price of $0.99. Both services, however, provide marketing advice and promotional opportunities. The land of indie self-publishing of e-books is alive and well and has allowed many aspiring authors to place their masterworks on the open market.

But, what if you prefer to see your book in printed form, as a paperback or hardback? What then?

Publishing as a P-book

In the good old days, an author would handwrite or type the first draft of a manuscript and then tout it around to find a traditional publisher to turn it into a proper book, or a literary agent who would do the touting for you. The publisher would then print and market the book through bookstore outlets such as Barnes and Noble, Waterstones, Smiths, and Foyles. Not any more. Book publishers are inundated with new manuscripts and it's virtually impossible to entice an established publisher to even look at your manuscript. You need to have already established yourself as an author (a classic chicken and egg situation), or be well known in some other field of endeavour, or 'know someone who knows someone', or just happen to write the most brilliant one-page covering letter and not-more-than-500-words synopsis that catches and holds the eye of an editor. I know. I tried it with one of my books, *Conversations*. The book was rejected by nineteen literary agents. There could be a hundred and one different reasons why the book was rejected and I'll never know which ones apply but it brought home to me just how difficult it is to find a traditional publisher.

THE MECHANICS OF CREATIVE WRITING

I attended a couple of masterclass seminars, organised by *The Guardian* newspaper, on the routes to finding a publisher for a book. The first masterclass was presented by two successful authors, accompanied by their literary agent; the second by a well-known publisher. Both classes stressed the difficulty of getting noticed. Anyone with the aspiration to become an author and who has access to a word processor can enter the market and, quite frankly, the traditional publishing houses have simply become overwhelmed with manuscripts. Additionally, or maybe ironically, the traditional hard-copy publishers are losing market share to online bookstores selling cheaper downloadable e-books. This adds an extra edge to the competition to publish in hard-copy form. Your book must exude a strong aroma of instant bestsellerdom before it even hits the desk of the agent or the editor whose job it is to make an initial accept/reject decision based on the covering letter, a synopsis, and usually the first three chapters.

All is not lost, however. You can self-publish your book as a p-book using online print-on-demand publishing and distribution services such as Lulu or Amazon's CreateSpace. I have familiarity with CreateSpace and this is the service I will concentrate on but before I get into the detail I have a warning: beware of vanity publishers.

A reputable publisher, such as Penguin Random House, Oxford University Press, HarperCollins, or Pan Macmillan, will not ask for any upfront fees if they accept you as one of their authors. The company will bear the cost of proofreading your manuscript, laying it out as a printable book, creating a front and back cover, and then printing and distributing the book to booksellers. The company makes its money through sales of the book, not through you. You will receive a royalty, of course, but the bulk of the money made from sales of the book goes to the publishing and printing company. That's the way it's always been, and still is, except for the vanity publisher and printing companies.

    A vanity publisher and printing company, let me call it a VPPC, is a new type of book publishing company. A VPPC will offer you a contract to publish your book but will ask for an upfront payment to offset the initial setup costs and subsequent marketing and distribution costs. I was approached by one VPPC—I won't say which one—and offered a variety of publishing packages ranging in price from the basic package at just under £1,000 to the top-of-the-range package at over £4,000. The price variations were accounted for by factors such as who creates the cover design, in which countries the book will be marketed, will the VPPC use a copy editor as well as a proofreader, will your book be distributed by third-party resellers, and so on. When I first received the offer, I was thrilled that, finally, someone had taken the trouble to read my book and wanted to become my publisher, but then I read the small print of the contract, researched the company and uncovered the world of vanity publishers. They do create a hard copy of your book but their success rate at marketing the book is low and, in fact, they are appealing to your desire to see your book in print no matter what the cost. You can do this yourself for much less money than that required by the vanity publisher by using an online on-demand publishing platform such as Amazon's CreateSpace service. Here's how.

    As I said, I have used Amazon's CreateSpace service to publish four of my books in printed form. Essentially, you do all the work traditionally done by a proofreader at a publishing company. CreateSpace does the printing on demand when a customer orders a copy of your book. On you is placed the burden of page layout, page number insertion, front and back verbiage—title and author, copyright notice, table of contents, and dedication at the front; about the author, other publications, upcoming book teasers, and index at the back. You will also be responsible for creating a decent-looking front cover and whatever you want on the back cover, usually a short description of the book (known as the blurb) and a short biography.

    None of this is difficult and, for example, CreateSpace offers a number of editable front cover templates to help you create your own eye-catching front cover. Here are some examples of the front covers I have created for my own books using CreateSpace's templates.

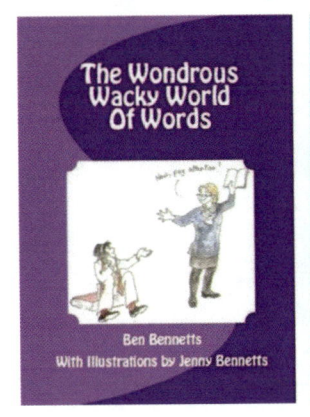

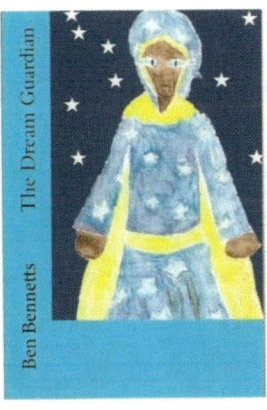

The covers are simple but effective and viewable even as thumbnails on, for example, Amazon's listing in the Books section.

Page layout may be a bit tricky, especially if you have included images among your text. You should avoid large sections of white space on a page and this may mean juggling blocks of text around or resizing images to fill up the white space. You will also need to pay attention to paragraph layout (block or first line indent), text justification, font selection and font size, use of special characters like the pilcrow symbol ¶ I've used (do you know where to find this symbol to insert in your text?), the position of images, page margins to allow for printer bleeding, headers and footers containing the book title, chapter sub-headings and page number, and so on. Services such as CreateSpace give you print page templates with correct bleed margins and advise on attributes such as font selection and size, image resolution and size, so help is available. In fact, I find page layout to be quite therapeutic, similar to assembling a photographic collage that is pleasing to the eye. I enjoy it.

E-book to P-book Conversion

If you plan on publishing your new book as both an e-book and a p-book, the question arises—which comes first: the e-book or the p-book? I've tried converting both ways and, without a doubt, creating the e-book first and then converting to a p-book is much easier than the other way round. Put simply, it's easier to add stuff than take it away and Styles comes into its own when you do this.

The layout of an e-book is simply one long piece of reflowable text with images centred and no distractions such as footnotes, endnotes, page numbers, page sizing constraints, and so on. Once the book looks acceptable on an e-reader, it's a relatively easy job to add the features that will turn the file into a printable set of individual pages. You may change the paragraphing style from block indent to first line indent, or the font type from, say, an e-reader-friendly sans serif font (Arial, Calibri, Tahoma) to a printed-page-friendly serif font (Georgia, Times New Roman, Palatino), but these changes are easily accomplished through Style modification.

Bookmarks and hyperlinks are invaluable aids to navigation in an e-book but have no place in a p-book. You should strip out the hyperlinks, or edit the hyperlink Style to ensure they are not printed in a different colour or underlined. This will render them invisible, the same as built-in bookmarks.

P-book images are normally of a higher standard than e-book images. I use a combination of PowerPoint and PaintShop Pro to create all my e-book images and I save at the p-book print standard—200 dpi, or higher, and properly sized in terms of width and height. For the e-book edition, I use the Compress feature in Word to reduce the resolution of all images down to 96 dpi as advised by, for example, Smashwords and KDP.

Finally and unfortunately, if you publish your book first as an e-book and then as a p-book, you will inevitably end up with two DOC masters. Not only are the layout and cosmetics (page number, header, footer, and navigation techniques) different, each version will have a different ISBN. Maintaining two masters of the same publication is a major pain. If you have an eagle-eyed granddaughter, as I have, who spots an error that has escaped your diligent copy editing, you will want to correct both versions.

I've never found a clever way of maintaining a single master file and then targeting it towards either the e-book or the p-book version. The differences in layout, in image properties, in cosmetics, and in the use of bookmarks and hyperlinks versus a standard index, are too far apart to allow a single retargetable master and so I live with two masters. As I said, it's a pain!

(^_^)

7. Creative Writing: Some Final Comments

    This book has been about the mechanics of creative writing. Mechanics is variously defined as *routine or basic methods, procedures, techniques, or details* (dictionary.com) or *the practicalities or details of something* (Concise Oxford Dictionary). The book is not about how to become a creative writer. I cannot teach you how to write creatively; how to arrange words so that they cause enjoyment or arouse some other emotion that will make a reader think of you as a creative writer. Nor can I teach you how to develop the interplay of characters in a novel; how to structure a piece of writing; how to use different literary conventions (styles to suit different book genres); how to structure descriptive dialogue, and so on. That's up to you. Your readers will be the judge of your literary creations and don't forget; beauty is in the eye of the beholder, or so the proverb says.

    But, I can make you aware of the tools and techniques to support creative writing. Like any craftsman who develops a creative skill beyond that normally expected, the tools to support the creation of the workpiece become the enablers for the creativity. I could not write blogs and books if I was not skilled in the many facets of Word. Nor could I create accompanying images if I was not well-versed in the use of PowerPoint and, to a lesser extent, PaintShop Pro. I need a good understanding of the so-called rules of English grammar while not being bound by pedantic adherence to these rules. I need to be able to navigate my way through various dictionaries and a thesaurus to support my choice of words. And, I need to be aware of the constraints of publishing in both e-book and p-book formats and be able to use the services available to me: Smashwords, KDP and CreateSpace. Once I have all this experience and knowledge under my belt, I can then indulge my passion for writing and let my flights of literary fancy soar and not be inhibited by a lack of understanding

THE MECHANICS OF CREATIVE WRITING

of the tools and processes that will turn my seething turbulent thoughts into something you, the reader, can read and enjoy.

This is why the book is about the *mechanics* of creative writing. Acquire the skills to use the tools and then let the creativity flow.

(^_^)

Further reading

English Grammar Books

The following books are in my bookcase. From time to time, I refer to them but I also exercise my own judgement. The year of publication is as per my copy of the book. If you decide to buy any of these books, check for later editions, including possible e-book versions.

Bennetts, B, *The Wondrous Wacky World of Words*, Atheos Books, 2015
Clark, J, *English Usage*, Harrap, 1989
Cutts, M, *Quick Reference Plain English Guide*, Oxford Press, 1995
Cappon, R J, *Guide to Punctuation*, Associated Press, 2003
Denham, T, *How Not To Write*, Piatkus, 2005
Fowler, H W and Gowers, E, *Modern English Usage*, Oxford, 1978
Gowers, E and Fraser, B, *The Complete Plain Words*, HMSO, 1973
Heffer, S, *Strictly English*, Windmill, 2011
Kamm, O, *Accidence Will Happen: The Non-Pedantic Guide to English Usage*, Weidenfeld and Nicolson, 2015
Parrish, T, *The Grouchy Grammarian*, Wiley, 2003
Partridge, E, *Usage and Abusage*, Book Club Associates, 1979
Ritter, R M, *The Oxford Manual of Style*, Oxford University Press, 2002
Rozakis, L, *Guide to Grammar, Usage, and Punctuation*, Random House, 1991
Strunk, W and White, E B, *The Elements of Style*, Macmillan, 1979
Truss, L, *Eats, Shoots and Leaves*, Profile Books, 2003

English Grammar Websites

There are many websites set up to help you sort out English grammar issues. I make occasional use of the following. The links were correct at the time of writing (2018).

Chicago Style Manual, http://www.chicagomanualofstyle.org/home.html
Christina Sterbenz, http://www.businessinsider.com/a-guide-to-proper-comma-use-2013-9
Daily Writing Tips, https://www.dailywritingtips.com/
GrammarCheck, http://www.grammarcheck.net/
Grammarly, https://www.grammarly.com/
Mignon Fogarty (Grammar Girl), http://www.quickanddirtytips.com/grammar-girl
Nick Stockton (on catching typos), https://www.wired.com/2014/08/wuwt-typos/
StackExchange, https://english.stackexchange.com/
The Writer's Digest, http://www.writersdigest.com/

... and more that come up when I google a particular grammatical problem.

Dictionaries and Thesaurus

Cambridge, http://dictionary.cambridge.org/dictionary/english/
Collins, https://www.collinsdictionary.com/
Dictionary.Com, http://www.dictionary.com/
Etymology Dictionary, http://www.etymonline.com/
Merriam-Webster, https://www.merriam-webster.com/
Oxford, https://en.oxforddictionaries.com/
Thesaurus, http://www.thesaurus.com/
The Free Dictionary, http://www.thefreedictionary.com/
Urban (Slang) Dictionary, http://www.urbandictionary.com/
Word Hippo, http://www.wordhippo.com/

Use them. Most of them are free to use.

Online Grammar Checkers

Ginger, http://www.gingersoftware.com/
Grammarly, https://www.grammarly.com/
GrammarCheck, https://www.grammarcheck.net/
Scribens, https://www.scribens.com/

Copyright Law

Fact sheet P-01: UK Copyright Law, issued April 2000, regularly updated,
http://www.copyrightservice.co.uk/copyright/p01_uk_copyright_law
http://iplegalfreebies.wordpress.com/2011/01/18/copyright-law-using-quotes-from-someone-else-in-your-book-blog-or-website/
Model release form, widely available but visit,
http://www.rps.org/MRF for an example.
Publishers Association, http://www.publishers.org.uk/
Society of Authors, http://www.societyofauthors.net/
Fair use of graphical images, https://www.rivaliq.com/blog/guide-copyright-fair-use-laws-online-images/

Clipart Libraries

Megapixl, https://www.megapixl.com/
Microsoft's Clipart Library, https://www.labnol.org/internet/office-images-usage/27823/
OpenClipart, https://openclipart.org/
Pixabay, https://pixabay.com/
Wikimedia Commons, https://commons.wikimedia.org/wiki/Main_Page
Flickr, https://www.flickr.com/

    ... and many more but check the copyright and royalty status of any clipart you download.

Online Publishing and Printing Services

Amazon's CreateSpace, https://www.createspace.com/
Amazon's Kindle Direct Publishing, https://kdp.amazon.com/en_US/
Calibre e-book manager, https://calibre-ebook.com/
Lulu, https://www.lulu.com/
Smashwords, https://www.smashwords.com/
Vanity Publishing, http://www.vanitypublishing.info/

(^_^)

Acknowledgements

With the exception of the two images based on Wikimedia Commons royalty-free graphics, and duly attributed, and the two front cover thumbnails (Kamm, McCarthy), all the images are my own work. Some of my compositions make use of clipart available in Microsoft's Clipart Library, and are © Microsoft. The cliparts are used under the terms of Microsoft's End User Licencing Agreement.

    I am also grateful to my wife, Carol, my sister, Maureen, and a long-standing friend, Paul, for their noble efforts copy editing this book. Each found different errors. Each suggested several improvements. And each gave of their time freely. The book is better for their efforts. Thank you.

(^_^)

About the Author
Ben Bennetts

Camber Castle, Royal Military Canal long-distance path, 2017

    I'm a retired electronics engineer. I write blogs and books and, before my knees wore out, walked long-distance trails with my wife, Carol. During my professional career, I authored two technical books and just under one hundred technical papers. Since retiring in 2007, I've written various books under my own name and two under the pseudonym of J C Pascoe. You can read more about the books on my website, ben-bennetts.com/books. The books are available as e-books on Smashwords and Amazon's Kindle Store, and as p-books in Amazon's Books section.
    Contact me at ben@ben-bennetts.com

(^_^)

THE MECHANICS OF CREATIVE WRITING

Atheos Books

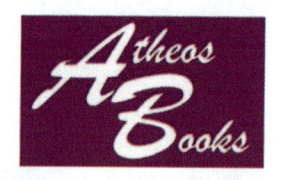

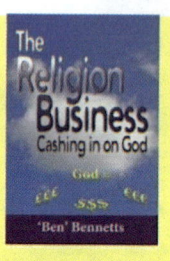

The Religion Business: Cashing in on God
2012, e-book and p-book

An atheist's view of religion

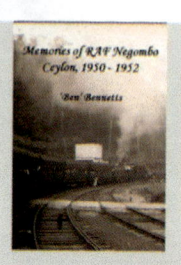

Memories of RAF Negombo Ceylon, 1950 - 52
(Assisted by Maureen Wyatt (née Bennetts))
2012, e-book.

My life as a young boy living on an RAF camp in Ceylon, now Sri Lanka.

On One Occasion... Ivory Tower and Road Warrior Stories
2013, e-book

Stories from my career as a university lecturer (Ivory Tower) and a travelling consultant in electronics (Road Warrior).

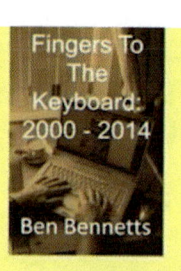

Fingers to the Keyboard: 2000 - 2014
2014, e-book

A collection of essays on many different topics.

THE MECHANICS OF CREATIVE WRITING

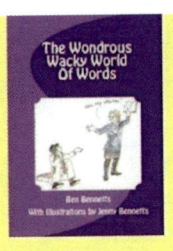

The Wondrous Wacky World of Words (with illustrations by Jenny Bennetts)
2015, e-book and p-book

An amusing look at the amazing different types of words in the English language.

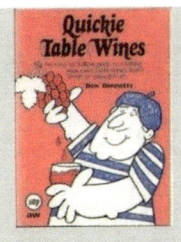

Quickie Table Wines
1977, republished 2015, e-book

Republication of the 1970s best seller about home-made wine making.

Tales from the Trails Part 1: UK Trails
2014, e-book

Stories from multi-day hikes along UK National Trails and other long-distance paths in the UK.

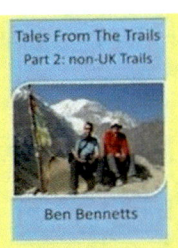

Tales from the Trails Part 2: non-UK Trails
2015, e-book

More stories from long-distance hikes, this time further afield (Nepal, India, Madeira, Spain and Switzerland)

THE MECHANICS OF CREATIVE WRITING

Conversations (J C Pascoe)
2016, e-book and p-book

A novel about a young university student (Abi) and an older divorcé (Gerry), the lives of honey bees, and lots of sex.
Note: sexually explicit and not suitable for minors.

Conversation Lite (J C Pascoe)
2016, e-book and p-book

As per *Conversations* but without the sex.

Fingers to the Keyboard: 2015 – 2016
2017, e-book

A collection of all my blogs published in 2015 and 2016

The Dream Guardian
2017, e-book and p-book

Stories told to Tommy and Nikki by Grandpa, the Dream Guardian.

THE MECHANICS OF CREATIVE WRITING

The Mechanics of Creative Writing
2018, e-book and p-book

Tools and techniques to support successful bish-bash-bosh writing.

(^_^)

Index

A

AutoCorrect. *See* Microsoft Word

B

Backup file, 9
Bish-bash-bosh, 21
Block paragraph style, 60
Bookmark/Hyperlink, 61
Bullet lists, 61

C

Calibre, 63
Caption, 62
Centred style for graphics, 61, 62
Clipart libraries, 73
Compress. *See* Microsoft Word
Copy editing (definition), 30
Copyright law, 50, 73
    70-year rule, 53
    Copyright definition, 51
    Fair use (graphics), 53
    Fair use (text), 52
    Graphics, 51
    Private edition, 51
    Private edition (fair use), 54
    Public-domain publication, 51
    Standard copyright clause, 55
    Text, 51
CreateSpace print-on-demand, 65
Creative writing, 2

D

Dictionaries, 72

E

E-book publishing
    Formatting text, 59
    Inserting graphics, 61
English grammar books, 71
English grammar websites, 72
Eonverye taht can raed..., 18
EPUB file, 58

F

Fact-check, 48
Fair dealings. *See* Copyright Law:Fair use
Find and Replace. *See* Microsoft Word
First line indent paragraph style, 60
Font selection, 61, 68
Formatting and inserting images, 62
Front cover design, 63
Further reading
    Clipart Libraries, 73
    Copyright Law, 73
    Dictionaries and Thesaurus, 72
    English Grammar Books, 71
    English Grammar Websites, 72
    Online Grammar Checkers, 72
    Online Publishing and Printing Services, 73

G

Grammar checkers, use of, 42
Grammarly, 42
Graphics print resolution, 62

H

Hidden bookmarks, 61

J

JPEG formating, 62

K

Kindle Direct Publishing, 57

M

Mark Coker, 64
Microsoft PowerPoint, 27
Microsoft Word, 21
    AutoCorrect, 22
    Compress feature, 62
    Find and Replace, 25
    Paragraph marker, 23

THE MECHANICS OF CREATIVE WRITING

Spellchecker, 22
Styles, 23
MOBI file, 58

N

Noah Webster, 17
Normal style for text, 59

O

Oliver Kamm, 12
Online grammar checkers, 72
Online printing services, 73
Online publishing, 73

P

PaintShop Pro, 28
Paragraph marker. *See* Microsoft Word
Personal Style Guide, 35
    Comma locations, 40
    Compare to versus *compare with*, 38
    Different *from, to, than*, 38
    Fewer versus *less*, 40
    -ize versus *-ise*, 35
    Lie, lay, lain versus *Lay, laid, laid*, 39
    May versus *might*, 38
    Model Release Form, 53
    Numerals and numbers, 35
    Only placement, 39
    Over-used sentence starters, 38
    Oxford comma, 39
    Passive and active voice, 40
    Punctuation in direct speech, 40
    Quotation marks, 36
    Repeated words, 36
    Replacements, 36
    Sentence and paragraph length, 36
    Sexists nouns, 39
    Synonymitis, 39
    That versus *which*, 37
    Use of contractions, 36
    Use of *italics*, 37
Photoshop, 28
Pilcrow symbol. *See* Paragraph marker
Planning, 8
PNG formatting, 62
PowerPoint. *See* Microsoft PowerPoint
Proofreading, 31
Publishing as a p-book, 64
Publishing as an e-book, 57

S

Samuel Johnson, 17
Smashwords, 57, 58
Spellchecker. *See* Microsoft Word
Styles, 23
    Block paragraph style, 60
    Centred style for graphics, 61, 62
    First line indent paragraph style, 60
    Normal style for text, 59

T

Table of Contents, 61
Text layout
    Block, 37
    First line indent, 37
Thesaurus, 36, 72

V

Vanity publishers, 65
Version control, 9

W

Web/Screen resolution, 62
Word. *See* Microsoft Word
Writing environment, 9

(^_^)

Made in the USA
Columbia, SC
06 May 2018